BEING ONESELF

BEING ONESELF

The way of meditation

Written and compiled by
F. W. Whiting
with members of
THE SCHOOL OF MEDITATION – LONDON

Published by THE SCHOOL OF MEDITATION
158 Holland Park Avenue
London W11
Tel: 01-603 6116

First published 1985
Second printing 1986
Third printing 1987
Fourth printing 1989

ISBN 0 9511056 0 4

Phototypeset in Baskerville

Printed and bound in Great Britain by
Biddles Ltd, Guildford and King's Lynn

ACKNOWLEDGEMENTS

Thanks are due to the following for permission to use quotations from the authors and works listed.

The Society of Authors: prose passage by John Masefield.

Mary Spain and Shepheard-Walwyn (Publishers) Ltd: *The Moment's Gold*, 1974.

Oxford University Press: *Some Sayings of the Buddha*, translated by F. L. Woodward and published in World's Classics, 1925; *The Meditations of Marcus Aurelius Antonius*, translated by John Jackson, 1906.

Wildwood House Ltd: *Lao Tsu: Tao Te Ching*, translated by Gia-Fu Feng and Jane English, 1973.

Faber & Faber Ltd: *The Ten Pricipal Upanishads*, translated by Shree Purohit Swami and W. B. Yeats, 1937; *Four Quartets* by T. S. Eliot; *Markings* by Dag Hammarskjöld, translated by W. H. Auden and Leif Sjöberg, 1964; *The Geeta*, translated by Shri Purohit Swami, 1935.

Macmillan, London and Basingstoke: *One Hundred Poems of Kabir*, translated by Rabindranath Tagore assisted by Evelyn Underhill, 1973.

George Allen & Unwin (Publishers) Ltd: *Plotinus*, translated by A. H. Armstrong.

The Daily Telegraph: article by Dr W. R. Matthews, late Dean of St Paul's.

Sidgwick & Jackson: *The Little Plays of St Francis* by Laurence Housman.

Penguin Books Ltd: *Prayer and Meditation* by F. C. Happold, Pelican Books, 1971, copyright David Happold; quotation from *Oxyrhynchus Sayings of Jesus in Mysticism: A Study and an Anthology* by F. C. Happold, Pelican Books, 1963.

William Collins: *The Gospel According to Thomas*.

Royal Society of Chemistry: quotation from Kekule Memorial Lecture in *Journal of the Chemical Society*, London, 1898.

George Braziller, Inc., New York: quotation from A. Kekule in *The Seamless Web* by Stanley Burnshaw, copyright Stanley Burnshaw, 1970.

J. M. Dent & Sons Ltd: *Beethoven* by Marion Scott, Master Musicians Series, 1974.

Fontana Paperbacks: *Varieties of Religious Experience* by William James, 1971.

Curtis Brown Ltd on behalf of the estate of Sarah Churchill: *A Thread in the Tapestry* by Sarah Churchill, copyright Sarah Churchill, 1967.

Robinson Books Ltd, London: *The Book of Mirdad* by Mikhail Naimy, Clear Press, 1983; *The One Work* by Anne Gage, published by Vincent Stuart, 1961.

Constable Publishers: *The Analects of Confucius*, published by Dover, 1972.

Mrs Laura Huxley and Chatto & Windus: *The Doors of Perception* by Aldous Huxley, 1968.

Simon & Schuster, Inc., New York: *Science and Human Understanding* by J. Robert Oppenheimer, 1966.

Methuen & Co., Ltd: quotations from Ralph Waldo Emerson, Plato's *Symposium*, St Peter of Alcantará and the *Tao Te Ching* in *Lamps of Fire*, edited by Juan Mascaró, 1961.

John Murray (Publishers) Ltd: quotation from *On Zen* by Dai-o Kokushi in *One in All*, compiled by Edith B. Schnapper, 1952.

American Heritage Publishing Co., Inc., New York: quotation from *Oratory on the Dignity of Man* in *The Horizon Book of the Renaissance*, 1961.

Apologies are offered to any copyright holders whose names may have been inadvertently omitted from the above list.

CONTENTS

Acknowledgements iii

Introduction vii

Chapter 1: The Strength Within 1

Chapter 2: The Inner Turn 5

Chapter 3: The Simple Technique 14

Chapter 4: States of Consciousness 19

Chapter 5: The Eternal Mystery of Time 26

Chapter 6: Human Relationships 36

Chapter 7: Aspects of Mind 41

Chapter 8: The Way of the Householder 48

Chapter 9: Man's Constant Search 54

Chapter 10: The School of Meditation 62

Appendices:

1. Questions and Answers 68

2. Individual Experience: some more examples 75

INTRODUCTION

In the beginning, when we were children, it was easy just to be. But the simplicity of being seems to disappear with the process of growth and learning. Inner delight and spontaneity fade as we move into adult life. Involvement with the activities of the world and the search for outer satisfaction can carry us away from ourselves. The source of contentment and quiet joy that lies within becomes covered over as life becomes more sophisticated. While the world is changing at an ever-increasing rate, instability grows. Many people find that the traditions which in the past provided a frame of reference no longer give the same sense of security. That insecurity increases as respect for law itself diminishes.

As always when society runs down, there are forces which arise to counter these adverse influences. One result has been the spread of ideas and practices from both east and west aimed at restoring balance to this disturbed world. Teachers from the east have attempted to remind the west of a way of life which is in keeping with natural law, and to reawaken awareness of the deeper aspects of man's nature, which lie beyond the pursuit of material progress. There has been a ready response to these reminders. Many people want to find a deeper significance to life, a point and purpose to their existence. They long to see peace restored to the world; and to see themselves and others pursuing their affairs with happiness and confidence. This has led to a wider acceptance of meditation as a method of restoring inner peace, freedom and contentment. But as alternative methods and techniques become available, questions arise: "If meditation is to allow people to discover what is already there, why so many different techniques?"; "Do different techniques produce different results?"; "Is there something which is common to them all?"; "Will meditation help me to know myself?"; "What does it mean in practice?".

Based on the experience of thousands who meditate, this book aims to answer such questions. Members of the School of Meditation were asked to give their own answers to the question, "What does meditation mean to me?". Collected here are some of their answers together with an explanatory text.

Meditation is not new. It has always been known in some form or other, the method varying according to time and place. In the Christian tradition, in Islam, and in the great oriental religions of Hinduism and Buddhism, meditation has played a vital part. Techniques of meditation vary, but at its deepest level meditation is one and the same for all. The importance lies in the depth of meditation; variation of technique belongs to the superficial levels of experience. Nevertheless, one must start at the surface level with a particular method.

The experiences recounted in this book come from people who practise a method derived from a long-established tradition. The tradition is centred in India; but this does not make it intrinsically "Indian" or "eastern", any more than the Galilean origins of Jesus make Christianity "middle eastern". It is a tradition which lies beyond any particular philosophy, religion or system. It does not relate to a particular creed; nor does it require those who meditate in accordance with its precepts to embrace, or to abandon, any particular creed. Thus, it can speak with integrity about the unity beyond the diversity of beliefs. It can also speak of the unity within the individual.

In everyone there is a depth of love and happiness, a potential of knowledge and intelligence rarely realized to the full. Meditation gradually releases this potential in the individual. It leads men and women to discover their own inner strength and capacity, and enables them more fully to participate in life. Efficiency in action, clarity of mind and warmth of heart are the hallmarks of those who meditate; powers which operate in the coherence of an increasingly united being.

Yet these are but partial benefits when compared with the great discovery of the unity behind all diversity. It is a discovery open to sceptic, atheist and devotee alike. For it is a discovery which illuminates the unifying principle in the great teachings of all times, in all places; equally, it provides for the many who have turned against all theory and dogma.

Each step must be checked and evaluated in practice, for meditation is practical, just as development of inner being is practical: proof rests in practice. All the ideas, explanations and examples in this book are therefore derived from the experience of thousands who meditate.

He that hath light . . .
may sit in the centre
and enjoy bright day.

John Milton, 1660

Chapter 1

The Strength Within

Meditation means strength — not from outside, which is where one always tried to get it before — but from the discovery of tremendous strength, calm and gentle, within oneself, which was always there. One cannot fall; the ground cannot be snatched away from beneath the feet. The limiting walls against which one kept banging one's head before are not there any more. One stands firmly and can look up and out and experience the world as it really is, and laugh — because there is no reason not to — and be free.

(Housewife)

Meditation has changed my life. Nothing drastic or dramatic. No flashing lights, no visions in the night. Nothing but a gentle, though seemingly inexorable, turning away from what was. There is a lessening of tempo, of temper; a gradual flowing towards people; an understanding of the underlying unity between me and all created things . . . An appreciation of what Matisse called "the lived-in silence of empty rooms" — the furniture speaking, the seemingly deserted room vibrant with echoes. Lying in the bath, one sees with sudden joy the harmony of simple forms — soap dish, jar of bath salts, tin of scouring powder — all bound together in a still life that any artist would take hours to arrange consciously. I am caught up in a timeless moment of recognition and joy. Yet I am just a middle-aged woman having a bath.

(Social Worker)

It's a foundation, a base, a calm centre from which I can do whatever needs to be done in the normal course of my life . . . I know that this foundation cannot be harmed. It isn't mine, so I need not fear that something or somebody will take it away from me; neither did I grasp it from somewhere outside myself, so I need not

1

worry about losing it. It is just there – not me, yet within me. It has been there all the time, really. Meditation did not add it to me, but helps to put me in touch with it.

(Computer Programmer)

A strength within oneself . . . A base, a calm centre . . . An underlying unity . . . A foundation . . . Do those who use such phrases about their experience of meditation refer to some part of the mind, or to a deeper level? What are these deeper levels?

All human beings accept that they have a body and a mind. Is there anything else, some faculty which is within practical experience and recognition?

In the beginning, all is simple. Everyone starts life as a baby. A baby is a compound of a mother and a father. It also has its own individuality, its own essential nature. A small child finds it easy to be natural; to be itself, regardless of its situation or surroundings. But many people find that in the process of growth and learning that leads to adult status they lose the ability to act naturally. They lose ease and spontaneity and the natural joy of childhood. Wordsworth is among the poets who have mourned this loss:

> Shades of the prison-house begin to close
> > Upon the growing Boy.
> But he beholds the light, and whence it flows,
> > He sees it in his joy;
> The Youth, who daily farther from the east
> Must travel, still is Nature's priest,
> > And by the vision splendid
> > Is on his way attended.
> At length the Man perceives it die away
> And fade into the light of common day.

("Intimations of Immortality from
Recollections of Early Childhood")

As he proceeds through life, man seems to lose touch with that which is natural to him. The most marked feature of this movement away from naturalness is the apparent disappearance of joy, of that inner happiness which characterizes the small child. Conscious of this loss, man seeks happiness outside himself in pursuits and possessions. These may bring satisfaction for a time, but rarely do they bring permanent lasting happiness. Many people remember that inner, lasting happiness of childhood; few acknowledge it as their birthright. John Masefield is one who did:

> It is difficult for me to describe the estatic bliss of my earliest childhood. All that I looked upon was beautiful, and known by me to be beautiful, but also known to me to be, as it were, only the shadow of something much more beautiful, very, very near, and almost within reach, where there was nothing but beauty itself in ecstasy, undying, inexhaustible.
>
> This feeling is probably present in most children; it was strong in me. I was sure that a greater life was near us; in dreams I sometimes seemed to enter a part of it, and woke with rapture and longing. Then, on one wonderful day, when I was little more than five years old, as I stood looking north, over a clump of honey-suckle in flower, I entered that greater life; and that life entered into me with a delight that I can never forget . . .

People who meditate begin to discover a deeper aspect of life and an ease, a joy, a happiness which is not dependent upon outer circumstances. This inner happiness comes from a strengthening of that which is natural in the person. It is experienced as within.

The strengthening of some inner aspect of being is followed by the first glimpses of powers lying latent in the nature of the individual. These latent capacities, in ordinary circumstances, cannot be fully expressed, if at all. They lie dormant, veiled by confusion of mind or lack of confidence. As the individual becomes aware of his own strengthening and of new capacities, he begins to meet again that inner happiness which he knew as a child; he begins to feel at one with himself and at one with the world.

To feel *at one* is very important. Man is, of course, one; he is whole and complete. Yet most people are rarely aware of experiencing unity within themselves. Especially in this age they feel uncertainty, they feel conflict within themselves, often with a duality of mind and body. Only occasionally is there experience of another aspect of the being, a glimpse of something which unites all the parts. When this happens, not only does the individual feel united within himself, but also in unity with his surroundings. Such moments may occur at any time; for city dwellers they are not uncommonly associated with the spaciousness afforded by the countryside, a seashore or a mountain top.

"We'll take you up to see the view," they said.
And so we journeyed through the Autumn rain,
The children wishing they had played instead;
Their weary parents trying to explain,
With fraying patience, how they ought to show
Their aunt the countryside. Five people, set
Apart by irritation, huddled low
Within the car. We got out on the wet,
Sweet grass, a very fractious cavalcade;
'Til, over-awed by space, dissension died,
And clouded eyes awoke to see displayed
The patient glory of the countryside.
As mortals changed, we stood in silence there;
And five were one, and one was everywhere.

(Mary Spain: *The Moment's Gold*)

Most of the time, people live in a world far removed from this sense of unity. Within and without, they experience mutliplicity and, often, conflict. Their reference points are continuously changing.

Meditation takes a person to the inmost part of himself, allowing him to experience that which is constant in his own inner essential nature and to discover the unity natural to him. Then body, mind and nature may work in unison.

To discover the wholeness, the completion, the unity, a man has to find the deeper levels of his being: and these appear, at first, to be within him, beyond mind and body. Only at a later stage does he see unity outside himself and everywhere, as he discovers that that which is in himself is in all men.

Chapter 2

The Inner Turn

To understand what meditation means, we must first throw aside prejudice: for meditation leads to knowledge of truth – a truth which is shrouded by a veil created by our own experience. Behind the veil, we may find, if we will, strength, peace of mind, calmness and the knowledge that all possibilities are within us and open to all; the knowledge that all is governed by a law of nature which acts unerringly.

(Architect)

Meditation is always there, a golden thread, connecting one to source. Through all the ups and downs of life, this thread is always there.

(Housewife)

I was brought up in the strictest religious faith and moral precepts; but in some way, it all remained outside me. It was "over there". When I joined the School of Meditation I remember a deep excitement at the personal, inward nature of meditation. This was something of one's own, something that was not dependent on temples or priests or sacred books or doctrines. Something one took everywhere, that was everywhere; and within oneself as well.

For most of my life I have been a student and an intellectual. I had a fervent belief in the supremacy of reason, the ability of science to discover everything, to solve everything, to achieve everything. Meditation (perhaps because it frees one, if only for a time, from never-ending thoughts) has given me an experience of something beyond and above the mind, something I would describe as spiritual awareness. It has enabled me to live with God, to be aware of God, in a way I cannot begin to describe, but which is nevertheless very real. This doesn't mean that I have come to despise science or reason. They have their place – but, for me, now, a subordinate one.

(Writer, Company Director)

5

When I came to meditation, I had for many years been seeking such a point of reference. Wide but superficial reading in philosophy, psychology, occultism and mysticism had filled my mind with ideas; but these seemed to float around, unrelated, disconnected and unproductive. I was like a man who had eaten a tremendous amount of food but who lacked the means of digesting and utilizing it. The hunger which powered this search seemed to come from an inner source. The need, as I see it now, was to establish a regular and sincere contact with the source of these early promptings. They were spasmodic and weak, seemingly at the mercy of external conditions. Meditation provided a very practical and immediate way of ensuring the contact was not lost, but was strenghtened and nourished. So the practice of meditation means to me, not a retreat from the reality of everyday things, but an ever-growing appreciation of what life has to offer.

(Teacher)

Meditation does not follow a particular religious system or teaching. It is related to the need of man to find himself and to find his purpose and place in the universe.

This need is constant. It has characterized people in all ages; and throughout recorded history it has been expressed in writing. The expression is varied; the purport is the same. Take the Dutch philosopher Spinoza, in the seventeenth century:

After experience had taught me that the common occurrences of ordinary life are vain and futile, and I saw that all the objects of my desire and fear were in themselves nothing good or bad, save in so far as the mind was affected by them: I at length determined to search out whether there was not something truly good and communicable to man, by which his spirit might be affected to the exclusion of all other things: yes, whether there was anything, through the discovery and acquisition of which I might enjoy continuous and perfect gladness for ever.

The need of man to find himself, and to know his purpose and place in the universe, is the scope of all religious and philosophical teachings. They describe the goal and they point the direction. The direction is

6

the same for all: the source of man's possibilities lies within.

Christian teaching speaks of it as the Kingdom of God. St Luke wrote:

> When Christ was demanded of the pharisees when the Kingdom of God should come, he answered them and said: the Kingdom of God cometh not with observation, neither shall they say, Lo, here, or Lo, there, for behold, the Kingdom of God is within you.

Other traditions point the same direction. The Buddha said:

> Be ye lamps unto yourselves.
> Be your own reliance.
> Hold to the truth within yourselves
> As the only lamp.

The Taoist teacher, Lao Tzu, is recorded as having taught:

> Without going outside, you may know the whole world.
> Without looking through the window, you may see the ways of heaven.
> The farther you go, the less you know.
>
> Thus the sage knows without travelling;
> He sees without looking;
> He works without doing.

In the Upanishads, a scripture venerated by as large a proportion of the human race as is the Bible, are the following words:

> God made sense turn outward; man therefore looks outward, not into himself. Now and again, a daring soul, desiring immortality, has looked back and found himself.

This is the direction of religious teaching: to turn back, to look within. This, also, is the direction of meditation.

Meditation has been likened to the shooting of an arrow. To make the arrow fly to the target, the bow has to be pulled back and back. An observer, not knowing, would say, "But that is the wrong direction. You need to push the arrow the other way". Not knowing, he does not realize that the potential energy lies in drawing back to the point of stillness and rest before one lets go.

7

The direction, this turn within, is understood not only by religion but also by philosophy. Marcus Aurelius, the Roman Emperor and philosopher, wrote:

> Look within. Within is the fountain of good, ready always to well forth if thou wilt always delve.

For him, the movement inward was a vital concomitant to the responsibility of governing a great empire. He also wrote:

> Men are continually seeking retreats for themselves, in the country or by the sea or among the hills. And thou, thyself, art wont to yearn after the like. Yet all this is the surest folly, for it is open to thee, every hour, to retire into thyself. And where can man find a calmer, more restful haven than in his own soul? Most of all, he whose inner state is so ordered that he has only to penetrate thither to find himself in the midst of a great peace – the peace that, to my mind, is synonymous with orderliness. Therefore, betake thee freely to this city of refuge, there to be made new.

Many references to the inner turn can be found in writings from those parts of the east where the practice of meditation is widely accepted as part of everyday life. Kabir, that rare poet and mystic, who united in himself both the Hindu and Islamic traditions, wrote:

> Be strong, and enter into your own body: for there your foothold is firm. Consider it well, O my heart! Go not elsewhere! Kabir says: "Put all imaginations away, and stand fast in that which you are".

More recently, in his book *The Evolution of Spiritual Man*, Sri Aurobindo, the Indian philosopher and teacher of this century, said:

> When there is a complete silence of the whole being, or a stillness behind, unaffected by surface movements, then we can become aware of a Self, a spiritual substance of our being, an existence exceeding even the soul's individuality, spreading itself into universality, surpassing all dependence on any natural form of action, extending itself upwards into a transcendence of which

the limits are not visible. It is these liberations of the spiritual part in us which are the spiritual evolution in nature.

The complete silence and stillness referred to here are of considerable significance to meditation. Their importance is stated by the Psalmist:

> Be still and know that I am God;

by Isaiah:

> For thus saith the Lord God, the Holy One of Israel: in returning and rest shall ye be saved: in quietness and confidence shall be your strength;

and by St Paul in advising the Thessalonians:

> . . . that ye study to be quiet.

From all sides comes this expression of the need for inner quiet and ways of discovering it. Take Plotinus, whose *Enneads* were written some 200 years after the birth of Christ:

> But how shall we find the way? What method can we devise? How can one see the inconceivable Beauty which stays within the holy sanctuary and does not come out where the profane may see It? Let him who can, follow and come within, and leave outside the sight of his eyes and not turn back to the bodily splendours which he saw before . . . Let all these things go, and do not look. Shut your eyes and change to and wake another way of seeing, which everyone has but few use.

As recently as October 1961, *The Daily Telegraph* published a similar message, from Dr W. H. Matthews, then Dean of St Paul's:

> Quietness is a scarce commodity in our civilization, and many of us find that to purchase it is beyond our means. Though less expensive, quietness of mind is no less difficult to secure, so that, in addition to the din of cars, planes and other assailants of peace, we have to endure the mental disquiet of the political and social unrest of a world in rapid change.

Yet one of the aims and rewards of the life of the Spirit is that "quiet mind" for which the Collect for tomorrow teaches us to pray. In this it agrees with the New Testament. In what is perhaps the first Christian letter ever written by St Paul, he urges his readers to "be ambitious" for another gift of the Spirit beyond the zeal and active charity which they have shown; let them strive for quietness of mind, which will enable them to look after their own business without distraction. [1Thes.IV,11]

This quietness of mind is the opposite of the fool's paradise. It is not terrified into stagnation, but active and alert. And in its quietness is its strength. Anchored on the inward peace of the Spirit, such a man will not dither in the face of emergency or despair or disaster, for his trust is not in luck, or chance, or in some future turn of events – it is in the Eternal.

This restless age needs to acquire quietness of mind if it hopes to escape catastrophe, and its physical restlessness may be partly a symptom of its mental and spiritual rootlessness. Who knows whether those who speed so senselessly from place to place may not be looking unconsciously for somewhere where there is peace – and not finding it.

Only through inner peace, we are told again and again, can there be personal experience of the great teachings given to man. The sixth-century "Desert Father", St Isaak of Syria, wrote: Make peace with yourself and heaven and earth will make peace with you. Endeavour to enter your own inner cell, and you will see the heavens, because the one and the other are one and the same, and when you enter one you see the two.

Laurence Housman wrote a play about St Francis of Assisi and attributed to him these words:

Human nature is like a pool of water, my Lord. Cast a stone therein, it goes rough and broken; stir it, and it becomes foul; give it peace, let it rest, and it will reflect the face of heavens which lie over it.

Whatever the idiom employed, the teacher, speaker or writer shows the way back to man's source, back to the seat of his possibilities and his fulfilment. There are many ways of finding this common source, some more difficult than others. The method of meditation has the advantage of simplicity; it is not peculiar to any sect or dogma, but may bring greater illumination to those who follow a particular philosophy or religion.

For example, the importance of inner quiet is stressed by those who describe the deeper levels of prayer. In his book *Prayer and Meditation*, F. C. Happold quotes Christian writers who describe the more profound levels of prayer life, using in particular St Teresa's description of the levels of prayer, which may lead from the Prayer of Inward Silence to the Prayer of Quiet.

> In the earliest forms of contemplative prayer the mental faculties are wide awake. One is still moving in a world of form and images; one is fully aware of one's individuality. Though one may be conscious of the Divine Reality, one is still also conscious of one's separateness. In the Prayer of Inward Silence and Simply Looking, one begins to move into a new world, on to a new plane of silence, where imagination and thought begin to fade out. The self begins to find itself released from the burden of time. The voices of the world begin to die away.
>
> Those who are capable of this Prayer of Inward Silence and Simply Looking and Waiting may, through grace, move into the Prayer of Quiet. With the Prayer of Quiet we reach the stage of true mystical prayer.

Happold then gives St Teresa's description of the Prayer of Quiet, including the words:

> The faculties are at peace and do not wish to move . . . The soul understands, with an understanding quite different from that given by the external senses, that she is now quite close to God and that, if she drew a little nearer, she would become one thing with Him by union . . . The soul understands He is here, though not so clearly. She does not know how she understands; she sees

11

only that she is in the Kingdom . . . Since the soul is so completely happy in this prayer of quiet, the will must be united during most of the time with Him alone who can satisfy it.

So meditation, which leads to inner quiet, may be a direct aid to those who follow a particular religion, but it has equal value for those who have no particular belief and no particular philosophy of life. Equally it can help those whose main interest is outer activity, for the direction of meditation is twofold. There is the turn within, to which end the technique takes the meditator to a place of peace and stillness, resting at the centre of being. The other direction is the turn out, when the meditator moves about activities. To use the analogy of the bow and arrow again: although one needs to pull back and pull back, the purpose of pulling back is to let go, so that the arrow may fly to the target carrying all the potential gained by pulling back. In the same way, the stillness of meditation is carried into activity; indeed, it is in activity that the greater discovery may be made. The Taoist teacher Ts'ai-ken t'an says:

> The stillness in stillness is not the real stillness. Only when there is stillness in movement can the spiritual rhythm appear which pervades heaven and earth.

In the words of the late Dean of St Paul's, quoted earlier, "quietness of mind is the opposite of the fool's paradise. It is not terrified into stagnation, but active and alert. And in its quietness is its strength.".

The move from meditation into activity is of great importance. For the fulfilment of man does not lie only in the inner depths of his being. It lies in every aspect of the universe around him. By first discovering the depths within, he may then discover the depths of existence everywhere. It is as if the inner Kingdom is both within and without. When, in 1945, thirteen volumes written on papyrus were found by chance in Upper Egypt, they included a *Gospel According to Thomas* ascribing to Jesus these words:

> If those who lead you say to you: See, the Kingdom is in heaven, then the birds of the heaven will precede you. If they say to you: It is in the sea, then the fish will precede you. But the Kingdom is within you and it is without you.

The same gospel says that Jesus spoke of the inner poverty that results if man does not find himself.

> If you [will] know yourselves, then you will be known and you will know that you are the sons of the Living Father. But if you do not know yourselves, then you are in poverty and you are poverty.

Many people who come to meditation say they come because of an inner lack, an inner need, an inner impoverishment. They find meditation replenishes this inner need and also opens up a way of self discovery. On the way, the validity and inner meaning of many teachings may be found in practice. These greater discoveries come gradually. First one starts with a simple technique.

Chapter 3

The Simple Technique

It is not sentimental or cerebral or learned . . . Each meditation practice is different. On one occasion, an important and determining memory may be released. On another, one may become more clearly aware of the nature of feelings and thoughts. But often one discovers a kind of quiet joy lying under anxieties or rages.

(Psychotherapist)

When I am able to come to the practice of being still and listening, the usual legacy of fragmented thoughts and ideas which crowd in, recedes; it is as if a burden drops away.

(Secretary)

The meditation period is, in a special sense, the centre of the day, when activities are just set aside and when, in T. S. Eliot's expression, one has the power to put oneself 'at the still point of the turning world', and to emerge refreshed. It may be the only time during the day when one really remembers oneself *and comes together as a whole. It may also be a period of peace and/or illumination.*

(Librarian)

Meditation is not a process of concentration or contemplation. The expression "meditating upon" is popularly used to imply the application of thought to a subject. In fact, the "thinking about" is more properly called contemplation; for meditation does not make use of thought processes in this way.

The difference is one of dimension. The thought processes may be considered as going on in a horizontal plane. They may encompass a broadening circle or a narrowing one, but they are limited to that plane. The method of meditation, in the same symbolism, takes a vertical direction, at right angles to and cutting across the thoughts of the horizontal plane. Just as the horizontal plane may be broad, so the vertical may be deep, dropping down through subtler levels of mental processes, down to a deeper level of being, beyond the movements of the mind.

To reach these deeper levels, one starts at the top of the vertical – which is where one ordinarily is – and follows the direction to stillness. In order to hold direction through the multifarious and distracting movements of the mind, a technique is necessary.

Techniques of meditation which do not use the thought process can be seen as relating to the senses. (Eastern teachings associate the senses with the elements space, air, fire, water and earth. Space is associated with sound, air with touch, fire or light with sight, water with taste, and earth with smell or fragrance). Increased awareness can result from techniques related to the five senses and the associated subtler elements.

For example, the sense of smell, although not highly developed in man, is brought into play by the burning of incense, used in many forms of worship and purification. Some techniques require the nostrils to be held with the fingers so that air passes alternately and regularly through each nostril. Others are based on letting the awareness be filled with the fragrance of flowers to the exclusion of all else.

Taste is often used in the subtle sense of "a taste for music, art, etc.". It denotes "a love for", and many meditative techniques use objects or persons which arouse love as an image either set before the meditator or held in mind. But this is only to have an object which produces a feeling of love, and by letting the love fill the awareness, objects and thoughts may be left behind, even the object of love itself.

Sight is utilized outwardly and inwardly by fixing the attention on special symbols, mandalas, or objects such as a flower or a candle flame. By concentrating the attention through the focus of sight, the meditator may be free of thoughts and images in the mind. Light is used by those who create in themselves an image of a light in the heart and focus their attention on that light.

Touch plays an important part in the use of the prayer wheel and the rosary, but touch is also associated with air, and several meditative techniques are based on focusing the attention on the breathing.

Meditation techniques using mantras utilize sound and listening, although some mantras are used in visual form. Mantras may be chanted out loud, but more subtle is the technique of sounding inwardly, with the sound forming a vehicle for the attention carrying it to the inner realms of being. Such techniques do not require a meaning or a thought process. Some meditative techniques require the awareness to be on pure listening but, without some vehicle for the attention, the movements of mind can easily distract.

There are other techniques, one of the most widely known being Hatha Yoga, which concentrate on physical posture.

Contemplative techniques using the thought processes may hold the awareness at the level of thought; techniques using bodily posture or movements may hold the attention on the body; techniques utilizing the senses which produce some inner experience may lead the meditator to be attracted to the experience. To find inner unity in the simplicity of pure awareness, it is necessary to go beyond body, beyond mind, beyond sensory experience. Techniques which reveal the inner peace and unity of oneself (as compared with those that aim to heighten outer experience) are directed towards releasing the attention from its attachment to thoughts, feelings and sensations so as to discover an inner realm of being and enlightenment. When the attention is caught by the movements of mind and the events of the world, it is possible to be pulled away from the centre point of being, to lose oneself and lose inner stability, balance and harmony. Meditation is to allow the mind to rediscover inner peace, freedom and happiness, so the technique is to guide the attention back home, back to the source of true fulfilment, home to oneself.

Meditators whose experiences are recounted in this book use a technique of mantra sound which is free of thought association, does not require imposed disciplines or concentration, and is so simple and natural that it is suitable for everyone. It cannot be learned from books and is always given orally in a traditional manner. The mantra sound acts as a vehicle or focus for the attention, drawing it from the grossest level of thoughts to subtler levels of conscious activity and, eventually, beyond movement to the stillness of inner being.

To have a meditative technique that brings one to inner peace and stillness is like having a well at the bottom of one's garden. No longer

16

is one dependent on outer sources of supply to slake one's thirst; one has a supply source in one's own domain. But to quench the inner thirst and find inner refreshment, one needs a technique to get the water from the well, such as a rope and a bucket. The technique is essential, but it is only a means to get to the source.

Inner peace, stillness and consciousness are in everyone, and it is natural for the mind to turn in this direction for rest and refreshment. All that stands in the way is the attachment of the mind to outer objects, images in the mind, worries, troubles, fears, anxieties, and so on. The simple technique of meditation releases the attachments, and then the mind naturally turns in the direction of peace. To find this direction there is no force, no effort, no struggle; rather it is a process of giving up, of letting go. But all our lives we have been taught to "do", to "try harder". True meditation is in the opposite direction, and the mind of man so caught in external pursuits and inner conflicts needs a technique of letting go, a technique of not doing. When, by virtue of the technique itself, the mind finds the natural inner direction, all that is needed is to allow it to maintain this direction without any doing; it is a practice of non-doing, a practice of letting go, a practice of coming to oneself. There is nothing added to this direction, which leads to deep meditation where differences in techniques have no relevance. Here one finds the ocean of being and one transcends movement of mind; thoughts, feelings and sensations are left behind. When mind has found inner refreshment, it is equally natural for it to return to the surface of being, the body senses and outer activity, but now with greater clarity, peace, simplicity and ease. It is like a swimmer who dives into the ocean and goes down and down quite naturally, rising again to the surface by the nature of the action.

Some people feel that meditative techniques are strange or "eastern". A true technique does not attach people to any particular background or system but frees them from limitations. As well as allowing them to find their own inner peace and happiness, it may help to bring a deeper understanding of their own cultures, teachings and traditions. Problems arise only when practitioners (and sometimes teachers) of meditation get caught on outer form and experience, creating all sorts of traps and artificial states. True meditation is beyond outer experience and any particular cult.

17

Some benefit will be immediate, from the very first session; but the deeper levels are reached gradually, as the practice progresses. The letting go is the key to penetration to these deeper levels, and many people need help, initially, to achieve this. For the most part, we have been taught to strive for what we want, so that it becomes habitual to struggle towards an end. In meditation, it is necessary to drop any effort that carries the quality of struggle.

The technique of deep meditation is practised for two short periods each day. When the practice is regularized and stabilized, it may take the meditator all the way to the unity within himself. Then he moves from himself; is happy in himself. He is not so dependent upon outer circumstances nor upon other people; yet neither is he separated from them.

He still has his own habitual tendencies and still has to face the circumstances of life which come his way; but differences and difficulties are seen in a new perspective, and he moves through them with greater ease and effectiveness. As the mind clears, potential increases, strength grows and the heart warms; so he helps himself and all associated with him. At the same time, his latent capacities find release, as he turns naturally and permanently to that which is true in himself and in all beings.

Chapter 4

States of Consciousness

My interest in meditation started when I was about 14 or 15. Life seemed vaguely unsatisfying then . . . I experimented with a yoga meditation technique although, because I was doing it on my own, without the support of a school, my practice was inevitably intermittent and somewhat desultory . . . I was swotting for my 'A' levels by this time and was pretty worried because I felt I didn't know anything. I decided to meditate for five minutes before I started work. After meditating for about a minute, something happened. A loud noise in the head, which had been so constant before that I had not even known it was there, was suddenly switched off. I felt relieved, happy and strong-minded. I knew I could go on meditating for so long as I wanted without being distracted. When I opened my eyes, the world seemed vivid, colourful and lovely. My usual short-sightedness had almost disappeared. I could read the French set-book that I was studying with remarkable ease and speed, and finished it in a couple of hours. The feeling of lightness and joy stayed with me for the rest of the day and the next, and I began to feel that all my problems were solved. All I had to do was to remain like this, which was the simplest thing in the world, and no trouble on earth could touch me. However, the day after, I began to doubt . . . and as soon as I did that, my habitual attitudes to life and ways of seeing returned. Intermittently, the perception I had had would come back for an hour or so a day, but after a year or so it stopped returning . . . Something very powerful within me wanted to forget. But I didn't forget altogether. When I left university, for some reason or other I came to London to work, and there I saw the School of Meditation's advertisements in the tube. I knew that was what I was looking for, and joined . . .

(Teacher)

Sometimes — not invariably — there is a sense of joyful serenity with a heightened awareness, a kind of vigilant attention which returns at intervals during the day.

(Housewife)

Meditation for me is a constant in a world of movement and change. It has gradually provided a still centre of reference and understanding within my being, from which I am able to move.

(Potter)

I believe that in meditation a door into a higher consciousness is pushed slightly open and one can glimpse another world of tranquillity and calm.

(Retired member of the British Council)

The subjects I teach are given new life by the increased conscious-ness and understanding that comes from meditation. Also, my awareness of the children and people I meet becomes more spontaneous, so that everything and every person in the world becomes more and more wonderful.

(Teacher)

Man is a conscious being. He has a higher level of consciousness than any other creature. Awareness is related to consciousness; and the extent and depth of a man's awareness depends on his state of con-sciousness. It is said of creative geniuses, mystics, saints and wise men that they have heightened states of consciousness; and many teachers and writers speak of developing these higher states.

All this remains something of a mystery for the average person. Yet meditation can give personal experience of increased conscious-ness.

There are three states of consciousness which are ordinarily experienced: sleeping, dreaming and waking.

Even in deep sleep there is some consciousness, for when we awaken out of deep sleep we *know* that we have slept well. Equally, we awaken to the cry of a child, to the smell of smoke, or to the sound of somebody calling our name. All this suggests that something is awake, is conscious, within us.

When we awaken from sleep, we move to a different level of consciousness, which carries broadening experience and awareness. We become conscious of this other world, in which we spend our waking days.

20

Between deep sleep and waking there is another level of consciousness, characterized by sleep with dreams. These dreams are related to the world we perceive in the waking state, but are often distortions of it, without its usual limits of time and space. Here again there is demonstrably a degree of consciousness: for there is something awake in the dreamer that can inform him that he dreams.

These dreams, however, do not stop when we wake up. We do not always acknowledge their presence, but in fact when we are busy recalling yesterday and imagining what will happen tomorrow, we are dreaming. We are certainly not facing present reality. Indeed, we can get up in the morning, wash, dress, have breakfast and be half way to work before we begin to notice our surroundings. Rarely are we wholly in the present.

The images that such dreams project in the mind can be pleasant; equally, when out of our control they can be very unpleasant. They can interfere with all activities, from concentration on study to peaceful sleep at night. As they deflect the attention from the realities of the present situation, they not only cause tensions and anxiety but also consume vital energy.

In contrast to this dream-dominated state, meditation leads the attention beyond the gross to a subtler level of mind, where there is less activity and fewer compelling images. Beyond that, it leads to a level subtler still, where there is no experience, no thought, no imagery. Yet this is no arid state of blankness. It is analogous to the condition of deep sleep, when the sleeper has no experience of images in the mind (although consciousness is present). In deep meditation also, the meditator has no experience of images in the mind, but is fully aware and conscious. Awareness at this level is not awareness of this and that; it is a condition of being at one with pure consciousness *which is always the same*. Led to the discovery of unity within, one begins to be truly at one with oneself.

Consciousness of this unity is known as Self Consciousness; and when the meditator reaches that, he begins to have a special inner knowledge of himself and of the people and events with which he is connected. Now he may begin to follow the direction of the great teachings which enjoin him, "Know Thyself".

Once this source of knowledge has been experienced, one needs to meditate regularly, to become stabilized in this inner unity. Then one begins to see the unity everywhere, as the presence underlying all relative experience. At first there are only fleeting glimpses of this reality; gradually, however, consciousness of the unity grows until one discovers the same Self in others. Here begins understanding of the words of the Upanishad: "Your own Self lives in the hearts of all".

As the flow of consciousness increases and strengthens, the three states operate at different levels: sleeping, dreaming and waking, each takes on a greater significance and potential. Waking begins to be wakening to a level of existence that is quite other than that of one's ever-changing thoughts, feelings and sensations; there is sight of a permanence in oneself and in others, which is neither personal nor subjective: and this permanence becomes a reality. One awakens to what is real, and also to what is unreal and transient; above all, the discovery that there is no lasting satisfaction in the transient. The permanence remains in the sleeping state, giving peace and unity. Dreams do not disturb and the sleeper just sleeps, with depth and refreshment.

With increased consciousness, the dreaming state has the potential of true creativity.

> Let us learn to dream, gentlemen. Then, perhaps, we shall find the truth . . . but let us beware of publishing our dreams before they have been put to the proof by the waking understanding.
>
> (A. Kekule: quoted by James A. Leuba in *Psychology of Religious Mysticism*)

This creativity will show in the particular discipline a man follows, and Kekule himself provided one of the best examples of "creative dreaming" in his account of how he discovered the structure of the benzene ring, one of the fundamental discoveries of organic chemistry. He had been working for some time on a textbook, without much progress, when – as he writes:

> My spirit was with other things. I turned my chair to the fireplace and sank into a half-sleep. Again the atoms flitted before my eyes . . . long rows, variously, more closely united; all in movement, wriggling and turning like snakes. And see, what was that? One of the snakes seized its own tail and the image whirled scornfully before my eyes. As though from a flash of lightning, I awoke; this time again I occupied the rest of the night in working out the consequences of this hypothesis.
>
> (Quoted in Stanley Burnshaw's *The Seamless Web*)

The master-composer, as well as the chemist, is familiar with the same kind of creative process. Mozart described it thus:

> When I am, as it were, completely myself, entirely alone and of good cheer – say, travelling in a carriage or walking after a good meal, or during the night when I cannot sleep; it is on such occasions that my ideas flow best and most abundantly. *Whence* and *how* they come, I know not; nor can I force them. Those ideas that please me, I retain in memory, and am accustomed, as I have been told, to hum them to myself. If I continue in this way, it soon occurs to me how I may turn them to good account, so as to make a good dish of it, that is to say, agreeably to the the rules of counterpoint, to the peculiarities of the various instruments. All this fires my soul, and provided I am not disturbed, my subject enlarges itself, becomes methodized and defined, and the whole, though it be long, stands almost complete and finished in my mind, so that I can survey it, like a fine picture of a beautiful statue, at a glance. Nor do I hear in my imagination the parts *successively*, but I hear them, as it were, simultaneously [*gleich alles zusammen*]. What a delight this is, I cannot tell! All this inventing, this producing, takes place in a pleasing, lively dream. Still the actual hearing of the *tout ensemble* is after all the best.

To these words, quoted in her book *Beethoven* (Master Musicians series, Dent), Marion Scott adds:

> If anyone wants to contend that it is impossible for a piece of music to be heard all at once, since music depends on its progress through Time, let them remember that Time is comprehended in Eternity. It is perfectly possible to transcend Time.

It appears that Beethoven also had access to a level of conscious activity with this extra dimension of time. He wrote:

> I see and hear the picture in all its extent and dimensions stand before my mind like a cast, and there remains for

me nothing but the labour of writing it down, which is quickly accomplished, when I have the time, for I sometimes take up other work, but never to the confusion of one with the other.

Mozart's precondition for this creative process was to be "completely myself". Beethoven also wrote of this primary need:

If heaven will only send patience until I can get abroad, I shall be able to get back to my real self again, which is the only possible happiness for men, and particularly for the artist. Patience, only, if I am denied anything else, I can still find myself again in nature; at one again in my heavenly art, too; Heaven's one true gift, this . . .

The sureness, the certainty with which those who have experienced this unity describe it carries conviction. Tennyson emphasized this aspect when he described:

. . . a kind of waking trance – this for lack of a better word – I have frequently had quite up from boyhood, when I have been quite alone . . . All at once, as it were out of the intensity of the consciousness of individuality, individuality itself seemed to dissolve and fade away into boundless being, and this is not a confused state but the clearest of the clear, the surest of the sure, utterly beyond words – where death was almost a laughable impossibility – the loss of personality (if so it were) seeming no extinction but the only true life.

(Quoted by William James in
Varieties of Religious Experience)

This heightened, or widened, state of consciousness gives insight into another level of existence – the only true life, says Tennyson. Like Tennyson, many writers testify to there being a life beyond change where there is universal joy and freedom, where the limits of the ego fade away. The consciousness is of that which is boundless being, everywhere the same; sure, clear, certain. The state of consciousness beyond the ordinary levels of sleeping, dreaming and waking has been called the Fourth State, Self Consciousness, Insight or Unitary Consciousness (as compared with the ordinary levels of relative

24

consciousness). Meditation gradually reveals this higher level, giving knowledge of inner unity. Then, from this point of unity, the consciousness may expand to give awareness of unity everywhere and in all things, which is a state of abundance sometimes called Cosmic Consciousness or Extended Consciousness. There are finer states still. For the purpose of this book, however, we have undertaken to remain in the realm of "ordinary" experience, which is easily demonstrable and describable. This is the area for which guidance is readily available for anyone who seeks it, provided only that theoretical ideas, imaginary visions and trance-like states are *not* the inquirer's principal interest.

Meditation is, above all, concerned with reality.

Chapter 5

The Eternal Mystery of Time

I find after meditating the whole scene has changed; the tempo has slackened, I can move at a more leisurely pace. Often a solution to a problem appears, or a different aspect of the same one, which enables me to see clearly. When this occurs, I feel a lightness of heart, something like joy. Tiredness often drops away and I can continue refreshed.

(Housewife)

All the time, when it was brought to my notice, one knew it was necessary to meditate; and that moment seemed to be the end of a search for something intangible.

(Company Director)

Meditation has increased my ability to work better — I seem to be able to focus my attention on the work, from moment to moment. I no longer daydream, nor need to as I enjoy life. Life has become an adventure again, as when one was young.

(Manager of Art Studio)

By meditating, one's mind is constantly turned to the present moment, so that when one is not meditating, a joy and fulfilment can be found in the present moment, during everyday actions such as walking or writing.

(Chartered Surveyor)

When I meditate, I experience a progressive release from my identity and my past. Thoughts, feelings and sensations become less compelling. There is ease and space and I may appreciate the presence of what I am . . . For me, meditation has importance beyond the events of my life. It provides confirmation that we are more than our bodies, our personalities, our acts and our experiences — and that the world is miraculous.

(Modern Languages Teacher)

Fundamental to many religions of East and West is the concept of eternity. Yet eternity is a word which for many betokens something impractical, something inconceivable and beyond experience, an idea without verification in life.

Meditation can help to unravel this eternal mystery of time. Of all the characteristics attributed to the practice, the change in the perception of time is most frequently mentioned. People say that they find there is more time or plenty of time; that the rush has been taken out of life; that they are brought into the present, where there is more clarity. They begin to experience a new dimension of time which, in the most practical way, gives a new dimension to life.

To understand such phenomena, we have to examine our ordinary concept of time. For most people, chronological time consists of a straight line, stretching from an incomprehensible past to an equally incomprehensible future. Somewhere along this line of passing time, we have our moment of birth and our moment of death. Between these two points lies our allotted span.

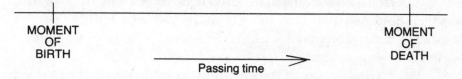

To us, time seems to pass as we move from our moment of birth to our moment of death. The past recedes, the future comes nearer. Time passes; our concept is one of passing time.

Somewhere along this line we are NOW.

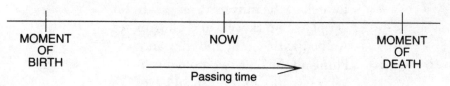

Some will be nearer the moment of birth, others nearer the moment of death; but wherever we are, exactly the same thing will have happened as these words have been read. Another moment will have slipped by, and we are in another moment of time. *Now* is a little further along the line. But the moment *now* is still *now*; it is still the present moment. Wherever we are on the line of time, it always stays

27

now. The line of time consists of a series of moments and each moment is *now*.

The journey from birth to death appears to be made up of a series of moments, which seem to come out of the future and to vanish into the past. Each moment is the present moment, *now*. A person who has tasted what it is to live in the present knows that time is always the same. It is always *now*. Such a person discovers a new dimension of time; a dimension of time which is other than passing time.

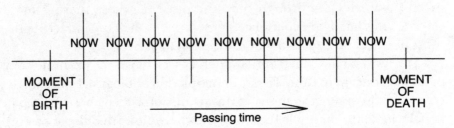

The vertical line represents the dimension of the moment *now*. The future comes to pass, but it is always *now*. *Now* does not pass.

A person who is always in the present exists in a dimension of time which does not pass, because it is always present. This time is not passing time. Compared with passing time, it belongs to another dimension.

The eternal quality of the ever-present moment *now* is described by Rupert Brooke in his poem "Dining-room Tea":

> When you were there, and you, and you,
> Happiness crowned the night; I too,
> Laughing and looking, one of all,
> I watched the quivering lamplight fall
> On plate and flowers and pouring tea
> And cup and cloth; and they and we
> Flung all the dancing moments by
> With jest and glitter. Lip and eye
> Flashed on the glory, shone and cried,
> Improvident, unmemoried;
> And fitfully and like a flame
> The light of laughter went and came.
> Proud in the careless transience moved
> The changing faces that I loved.

'Til suddenly, and otherwhence,
I looked upon your innocence.
For lifted clear and still and strange
From the dark woven flow of change
Under a vast and starless sky
I saw the immortal moment lie.
One instant I, an instant, knew
As God knows all. And it and you
I, above time, oh, blind! could see
In witless immortality.
I saw the marble cup; the tea
Hung on the air, an amber stream;
The painted flame, the frozen smoke.
No more the flooding lamplight broke
On flying eyes and lips and hair;
But lay, but slept unbroken there,
On stiller flesh, and body breathless,
And lips and laughter stayed and deathless,
And words on which no silence grew;
Light was more alive than you.
For suddenly and otherwhence,
I looked on your magnificence.
I saw the stillness and the light,
And you, august, immortal, white,
Holy and strange; and every glint,
Posture and jest and thought and tint
Freed from the mask of transience,
Triumphant in eternity,
Immote, immortal. Dazed at length
Human eyes grew, mortal strength
Wearied; and Time began to creep.
Change closed about me like a sleep.

This poem describes the eternal moment *now*, which is a dimension of time other than passing time. Yet this eternal ever-present moment *now* cannot be a series of moments, if it is a dimension of time which always remains the same. The present moment *now* is always *now*: so there cannot be a series of lines of time, or else they would be different times. If our concept of passing time is considered as a cycle, the present moment *now* can only be represented as ever the same, in a dimension other than that of passing time.

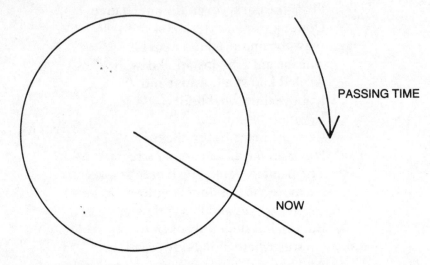

Everything that man observes in his universe appears as cyclic. The planets rotate, the galaxies rotate, the electrons round their nuclei rotate. We live by the regular cycle of days, months and years, and nature's cycle of seasons. If tea-time is 4 o'clock today, tea-time will be 4 o'clock tomorrow, day by day, in a cycle of time.

This is more generally acknowledged in the East, where it is usual to consider man's life as a cycle. In the West, where our criteria tend to relate to what we experience, this cyclical concept is not so easily accepted. Yet we do have personal experience of the cycles of days, months, seasons and years.

Although time may be seen as a cycle, it is still apparently made up of a series of moments, all of which are the present moment *now*. If it is considered as a cycle, then the dimension of time, through the ever-present moment *now*, can be likened to the radius of a circle – the circle of passing time, with the revolving radius giving a series of moments of time, all of which are the present moment *now*.

The eternal quality of the ever-present *now* was described by the nineteenth-century English novelist and writer on the countryside, Richard Jefferies:

It is eternity now, I am in the midst of it. It is about me in the sunshine; I am in it, as the butterfly floats in the light-laden air. Nothing has to come; it is now. Now is eternity; now is the immortal life. Here this moment, by this tumulus, on earth, now; I exist in it. The years, the centuries, the cycles are absolutely nothing; it is only a moment since this tumulus was raised; in a thousand years more it will still be only a moment. To the soul there is no past and no future; all is and will be ever, in now.

In the ever-present moment *now* is that which is constant, eternal, ever the same. Yet people rarely live in the present. As Jonathan Swift says:

Very few men, properly speaking, live at present, but are providing to live another time.

People are rarely aware of the present moment *now* and what is happening in this moment. They spend much of their life caught on the turn of passing time, recalling past events and imagining what may happen in the future. Such reconstructions and forward plans may have value; but if a person is caught by them, and the attention is carried away from the present, all the freshness and reality of *now* is lost. In contrast, to live in the present is to discover the value, the dimension, the constancy of *now*. As T. S. Eliot wrote:

Time past and time future.
Allow but a little consciousness.
To be conscious is not to be in time
But only in time can the moment in the rose-garden,
The moment in the arbour where the rain beat,
The moment in the draughty church at smokefall
Be remembered; involved with past and future.
Only through time time is conquered.

Another modern comment comes from Sarah Churchill in her biography of her father, Winston Churchill. In *A Thread in the Tapestry* she described how:

One night we were sitting after dinner looking across the lake. The silence, broken only by the goat bells, the stars dimmed in the velvet of the night by the peaceful flaring of his cigar. Suddenly he said: "Out of a life of long and varied experience, the most valuable piece of advice I could hand on to you is to know how to command the moment to remain".

People who meditate come to live more and more in the present moment. Meditation does not limit the capacity to recall past events or to consider future actions; but it enables one to consider them from the present, from where one is. In the present moment, everything appears new, fresh and clean; things are seen to be as they are. This new dimension of time adds a new dimension to passing time.

Meditation can also change one's sense of time. It cannot, of course, change chronological time. Chronological time and the sense of time are not the same. The individual's sense of time is based on the biological clock systems, which science has revealed to be present in the body. These internal biological clocks are numerous and varied. There are those which relate to the breathing and the heart-beat, the cycles of which may vary considerably as between, say, the condition obtaining in meditation and the condition of excitement or panic. Then there are the cycles connected with the lifetime of each particular organ in the body. At certain ages, human beings become very aware of change in their inner clocks, as one or another gland or process works differently or reaches the end of its useful working life.

To synchronize his daily activities with those of the rest of the world, a man normally uses not his internal clocks but an external measure of chronological time, like a clock or watch, or some other convenient mechanical device, based on the rotation of the earth. The period of that rotation is divided into 24 segments called hours. A clock based on hours enables a man to relate his movements, not only to those of his fellow men, but also to the movements of the earth in relation to the sun. So, when he looks at his watch and thinks, "Four o'clock: time for tea", he is really referring to the earth's cycle of time. This provides him with a constant reference of time.

The comparative stability of the earth's time shows up the variability in the sense of time from one human being to another. People who have been involved in car accidents, for example, frequently speak of an awareness that the accident was about to happen and of how time changed, so that all the events seemed to take place in slow motion. In such a situation, when there is apparently plenty of time to observe what is happening, it is often found that there is a complete absence of fear or apprehension – until the event is over and the usual sense of time has returned.

It is also a matter of common experience that on some days we seem to have more time than on others. There is less rush and we get more done.

Again, as we grow older, our sense of time changes markedly, to give the impression that there is less time. As children we mark our existence in hours, and two weeks to Christmas seems an eternity! For the adult, however, as time revolves with ever-increasing speed, we note time in days, weeks or months, until even a year can slip past all too quickly.

Another factor in the variation of man's sense of time is that we cannot know whether ours is the same as that of anyone else. We have no means of comparing whether an hour for me is the same as an hour for you. The fact that we need our watches so much suggests that it is not. The comment "Meet you in an hour's time" would not bring the desired meeting-point if all clocks and watches were removed and people had to rely on their innate sense of time. Indeed, all the jokes about women keeping men waiting may relate to a general difference in the sense of time, or perhaps to a tendency on the part of women to rely more on inner sense than on mechanical devices.

The present moment *now* always stays the same; but the sense of passing time varies, and people live in different cycles of time. This is graphically illustrated by the experience of the man who was standing in a building when it was hit by a bomb. He saw a heavy beam falling directly on to another man. The beam crashed in a split second and, to his amazement, it seemed to pass completely through his colleague, finishing with the beam resting on the floor and the man standing on the beam. To, the colleague, the experience was quite different. He said that he had a sense of the beam falling and seemed to have plenty of time to move out of the way and, once the beam had fallen, to step back on to it, into his original position. These differing descriptions of the same event indicate that the two men were experiencing, in an emergency, different dimensions of time.

The variations in the sense of time can be expressed thus, diagrammatically:

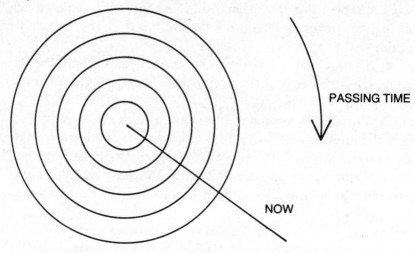

The present moment *now* stays the same; it is the sense of passing time that varies. It is easy to see, on the diagram, that the turn of the outer circle must be more rapid than the turn of the inner circle, just like a bicycle wheel which turns more rapidly at the circumference while the centre remains still. Similarly, as we grow older, we experience time passing more quickly; the cycle which is our sense of passing time moves out from the centre.

Within everything that turns, there must be a still centre, "an inmost centre", as Robert Browning said, "in us all, where truth abides in fullness". Meditation brings man nearer to that still centre, the still centre of his being.

So it is that, in relation to time, meditation produces two effects. First, it brings a greater awareness of the ever-present moment, *now*, with the ability to live in the present moment and that clarity which enables one to see things as they are. Then, with regular practice, as a man is drawn nearer to the still centre of his being, he gains freedom from the increasing pace and pressure of the daily round, and he tastes of the abundance of time.

This is a matter of personal experience, not theory. With this experience, a deepening appreciation grows of the words of the wise, who have described the different aspects of time.

The apprehension of time is caused by the perception of the changing instant, the apprehension of eternity by that of the enduring instant . . .

That was the way in which St Thomas Aquinas expressed it. Seven hundred years later, Mikhail Naimy puts it like this:

The wheel of Time revolves in the voids of space. Upon its rim are all the things perceivable by the senses, which are unable to perceive a thing except in Time and Space. So things continue to appear and disappear. What disappears for one at a certain point of Time and Space appears to another at another point . . . For motion in a circle can never reach an end, nor ever spend itself. And every motion in the world is a motion in a circle.

Shall Man, then, never free himself of the vicious circle of Time? Man shall, because Man is heir to God's holy freedom.

The Wheel of Time rotates, but its axis is ever at rest . . . In the axis all is peace. On the rim all is commotion. Where would you rather be? I say to you, slip from the rim of Time into the axis, and spare yourself the nausea of motion. Let Time revolve about you; but you revolve not with Time.

The Book of Mirdad

Chapter 6

Human Relationships

I have therefore become more tolerant and more understanding, loving and forgiving.

(Dormitory Attendant)

Gradually, greater sympathy for and understanding of other people have developed; and when I do lapse into negative or antagonistic attitudes of mind, I can at least see myself doing it, and some part of me is able to view the situation in a more detached manner than was possible before I learned to use my mind constructively. I don't have to act on every feeling which I experience.

(Teacher)

One is aware in meditation that all is one. In the daily routine, this understanding that there is no separateness makes one look at all creatures and things in a new light. I have experienced the underlying harmony in situations where, previously, I would have been emotionally involved and suffered stress and strain.

(Housewife)

My husband and I both meditate. This has increased our understanding of each another and has thus deepened our relationship.

(Secretary)

We live in a world of relativity, where everything is in flux and motion. It has been seen, for example, how we may relate to one of a number of time-scales at any given moment. Similarly, we may relate to one of a number of scales of values at any given moment. It all depends on the state of mind.

At their simplest, these relative values are a reflection of what the individual has acquired through habit and upbringing. They tend to reflect what he likes or dislikes, what elates or depresses him, of what he approves, and of what he disapproves. In this way, life becomes a series of dualities; and when he thinks about something, the mind almost automatically starts by presenting the opposite. Thus, if he stands for black, then white will come in, as something to be rejected or opposed. If he stands for east, then west appears in the mind, and an appropriate attitude is adopted. Similarly, "man" brings in "woman", "management" brings in "workers", "government" brings in "unions". In other words, hidden in our thinking about relationships, almost inevitably, is the concept of opposition.

The idea of opposition can bring conflict in society and in the individual. But there are few who have not glimpsed the underlying unity. It is often experienced quite unexpectedly, when one catches the eye of a complete stranger and, in that moment, recognizes something in the glance of the other, so that there is a shared knowledge of that which is the same.

When two people fall in love, they are joined together by a more intense – and perhaps lasting – experience of the same kind. In this communion they experience a unity which is greater than either of them, and which has no bounds. Not only does all the world love a lover: a lover loves all the world – so long as acknowledgment of the all-embracing unity remains. Under the influence of this unifying force of love, everything seems fresh and new and light.

Why does this state so rarely last? It is because one or the other or both soon miss the unlimited unifying force and instead start to look for something limited and personal. They attribute the love to themselves or to the other person, and cease to acknowledge that it is larger than both. They forget the pure, unselfish quality of the emotion, love, and confuse it with their ever-shifting feelings.

The emotion, love, is constant and never-changing; that is its hallmark. One of Shakespeare's sonnets expresses it precisely:

> . . . Love is not love
> Which alters when it alteration finds,
> Or bends with the remover to remove:
> O, no! It is an ever-fixed mark
> That looks on tempests and is never shaken . . .

The constancy of true love brings a communion deeper than any difference or difficulty. Communion and communication are words which derive from the concept "in common". It is ironical that in an

37

age when techniques of communication are so highly developed and when so much is said about the need to communicate, individuals but rarely communicate with one another at all. Where communication fails, it is through the loss of any deep sense of what people have in common. They can spend whole days without really meeting anyone else; members of a family can exist in the same house with nothing more than superficial encounters; and society, the larger human family, can operate with its members in a world of separation. "Who is incapable of communion", said Socrates, "is also incapable of friendship". Falling out of love, we miss what we have in common. Missing what we have in common, we see only differences and opposites.

The family is the unit of society. Yet so many married couples find that, at least for part of their lives, they lose the sense of unity and understanding which brought them together. The differences between the sexes are a source of delight when supported by unity; but they become differences barely to be tolerated when unity disappears, and insufferable when seen as a source of opposition. This is the fate of many marriages: with feelings, thoughts and actions alike expressing friction and misunderstanding.

When through meditation unity is rediscovered, a new point of reference appears in family relationships. Man and wife become more aware of that which is the same, beyond the differences. The differences themselves, when experienced through knowledge of unity, make for attraction and understanding. The couple find in practice that, gradually, they begin to act as though both partners were of the same family – the family of mankind. This is not a theoretical proposition; it happens slowly but spontaneously and naturally, and often may come about even if only one of the partners meditates. There can be growth in mutual understanding, greater consideration for and acceptance of the other, and a gradual reduction in friction.

Of course, habits remain – or are likely to, for at first the extra energy released by the practice of meditation may power the habitual reactions. However, if the practice is regular and deep, gradually establishing inner unity, then although the habits remain they become less infuriating, less likely to spark off action and reaction, less likely to produce that negative flow which can lead to intellectual withdrawal and emotional outburst. Frictions still occur, but less frequently. Emotions flow, but more positively, and the couple may grow in love and understanding.

As Jo Coudert said, "The arithmetic of love is unique: two halves do not make a whole; only two wholes make a whole".

Family relationships may be easier and more fruitful after reaching the deeper levels in meditation. The same growth in ease and unity may take place in business and community relationships, leading to a reduction in non-communication, isolation and loneliness.

One way in which people combat their loss of wholeness and stability is by resort to drugs. The social concern about the increase in drug dependence and its effects on human relationships merits special consideration. A distinction should be drawn here between drugs given by a doctor on prescription and drugs like marijuana and heroin. Many items in the first category are tranquillizers, designed to reduce stress and anxiety states. Others may be stimulants, prescribed to remove depression, or hypnotics to deal with insomnia.

The increasing demand for such medicines in the "developed" countries of the world reflects the widespread lack of inner rest, stability and confidence. Indeed, it would seem that the more sophisticated a society becomes in terms of its material wealth, the less developed is the inner life of its individual members.

Meditation can give inner rest, greater stability and increased confidence, with a consequent reduction in the need for medicinal drugs. It is not suggested that people who have long taken tranqillizers and such drugs should abandon them without consulting a doctor. What is being postulated is that the growing dependence on drugs, in the community at large, could be reduced through meditation.

When it comes to that other category of drug – LSD, heroin, and the like – addiction develops for a variety of reasons. Behind these reasons there is invariably one of two simple factors. Either there is a desire to escape from the experience of life as it appears, or there is a desire to gain experience of an existence which is greater and deeper than ordinary life.

Those who take to drugs as a way of escape usually finish on the hard drugs, such as heroin, becoming completely dependent and suffering all the tortures of drug addiction.

Those who take soft drugs – particularly when young – mainly seek experience beyond ordinary sense perception. It was Aldous Huxley who first gave popular publicity to the fact that certain psychedelic substances could extend perception beyond the ordinary limits of the five senses. In his book *The Doors of Perception*, he recounted his own experience with the drug mescalin.

Many young people believe that there must be a level of existence beyond that of their everyday experience; and they are convinced that the standards of their elders are superficial, selfish and materialistic. Such reasoning is the prelude to many experiments with LSD or marijuana and, indeed, the resultant "trip" may show something greater or deeper, beyond ordinary perception. Experience of this sort lies behind the moves to secure the legalization of drug taking.

Socially acceptable or not, drug trips nevertheless can have dangerous and frightening effects. Any foreign substance with such physiological power must have side effects if taken into the body – effects which are difficult to calculate. If the desire to move beyond the limits of ordinary perception is natural to human beings, then reason suggests that there must be some way of satisfying this desire, without the risk of hallucination or other damage to the mind and emotions. Meditation provides such a way, as has been proved by the many regular soft-drug takers who, when meditating regularly, find they do not need their drugs.

Breakdown of family life, increasing social conflict, growing drug addiction and the consumption of tranquillizers, hypnotics and stimulants all reflect an inner disquiet and dis-ease. A method that reduces the inner distress must reduce outer dependence and bring great peace to the world. For world peace, the individuals of the world must first be at peace with themselves.

> With the mind right the individual self comes into flower. With the self in flower the family becomes an ordered harmony. With the families ordered harmoniously the state is efficiently governed. With states efficiently governed, the Great Society is at peace.
>
> (Confucius: *The Great Learning*)

Chapter 7

Aspects of Mind

I tend to be introverted and thoughtful. Sometimes, I have felt my mind has too much energy: everything is noticed – a facial expression, a sigh, a leaf falling from a branch. My mind, continually analysing, seems to become tense like a clenched fist. Meditation has helped me to learn to relax, physically, mentally and spiritually. I seem to have an increasingly deepening awareness of life, without being overwhelmed or frightened by it . . . I have also noticed that my mind is becoming more discriminating about which thoughts to "think out". Now, any thoughts which are harmful or full of anxiety I gently "let go". This has meant an enrichment of my spiritual life.

(Sales Manager – Publishing)

I have found that I have been given the power to understand to a growing extent the true nature of people, things and happenings around me. Most of us know that the life we lead and our understanding of it is so limited, biassed and distorted as to be more a dream world than reality; and we rarely get a glimpse of the real existence beyond. Meditation is the door to truth.

(Company Director)

Meditation is not a physical exercise but an exercise of the mind and of those parts of existence which are subtle. Through meditation, I have a better knowledge of the mind and of the relationship of the mind to experience. I have learnt for the first time what is loyalty and the requirements of selflessness. Meditation has not prevented me from being offended or depressed, but it has given me an insight into the origins of these emotions and how I might be free of them. I believe that this knowledge is latent in everyone but that before it can be clearly known one must have a key. For me that key is meditation.

(Solicitor)

Modern science concerns itself almost exclusively with the physical world and its instruments measure physical phenomena. To apply scientific instruments to meditation, therefore, means only that some effects in the physical body of the meditator can be measured. Limited as they may be, such measurements are of interest.

One of the first research groups, including psychiatrists, doctors and technicians among its members, carried out experiments in London on people while they were meditating. They found that there was a general reduction in the rate of breathing and a slower heartbeat. The basal metabolic rate decreased by as much as 40 per cent. The increase in the alpha rhythm of brain impulses indicated a state of deep rest, but with inner awareness.

Findings of this sort have been published in a number of scientific and medical journals after studies of different types of meditation, pricipally Zen and transcendental meditation. The indications point in the same direction. There is a reduction in oxygen consumption and metabolic rate, which together evidence a deep state of rest, more profound than that of sleep or hypnosis. There is also proof of reduction of anxiety; this can be measured by skin resistance, which decreases in conditions of stress and increases during meditation practice. Another measurable factor is the blood lactate level, which is high in anxiety states, but shows a marked reduction during meditation.

Although electroencephalograph readings indicate a restful state, they also register inner alertness. This condition is emphasized in post-meditation tests, where increased speeds of reactions are registered. Recall tests further show that, after meditation, meditators perform better with the mind, and learn more quickly than those who do not meditate. There is now extensive literature available on the results of tests on meditators which have confirmed and expanded these early findings.

Recent investigations into consciousness and the functioning of the brain help to explain how meditation produces some of its effects. When people meditate, they say they find peace of mind. They speak of experiencing layers of mind: the first in noisy motion, the next a little quieter; the next, quieter still, with deepening awareness, insight and existence beyond the ordinary level of mind.

For a long time it was thought that while we had two legs, two arms, two lungs, two ears, two eyes, we only had one brain. But now researchers conclude that we have two brains rather than one and that man makes excessive use of one brain and neglects to use the other. This does not mean that man has two minds, only that the brain as the physical organ of mind has a dual function.

Scientific investigators interested in consciousness and the mind have studied the brain and its cerebral hemispheres. In structure and function the two hemispheres of the brain mirror each other with a full set of centres for sensory and motor activity of the body: muscular movement, vision, hearing, etc. Each hemisphere of the brain is mainly associated with one side of the body, the right brain controlling the left side of the body and the left brain controlling the right side. Each hemisphere's influence, however, is not always restricted in this way: when an area in one hemisphere is damaged, the corresponding area in the other hemisphere can take over its work to control the functions involved on both sides of the body. In other words, either half of the brain can to a great extent serve as a whole brain.

The two halves of the brain are linked together and normally function as one organ. They are united not only by the common stem of the spinal cord but also by bundles of nerve fibres connecting parallel centres in the two hemispheres. The most prominent of these connections is through the great cerebral commissure or *corpus callosum*.

To the surprise of brain surgeons, it was discovered than when the *corpus callosum* was cut, the severing of fibre connections between the cerebral cortices produced little or no noticeable change in patient capacities. In recent years, however, experiments have shown that a split brain (which may be the result of an abnormality, an accident or surgery) is not entirely normal in its function. It was discovered that what was learnt by one side of the brain was not transferred to the other. In fact, the two sides could learn diametrically opposed solutions to the same problems. It was as though each hemisphere was a separate mental domain operating with no awareness as to what was going on in the other hemisphere. It was as if the experimental subject had two entirely separate brains. Workers in this field have concluded that the two brain hemispheres are for the most part separate realms

43

of knowledge and awareness and that active attention by one hemisphere tends to weaken the attention of the other. When the brain is bisected, what results are two separate mental units, each with its own memory and its own will competing for control over the organism. These same workers have suggested that the intact brain could well be subject to conflicts that are attributable to the brain's double structure. Certainly this would seem plausible if they are not working together, and could well explain many of society's ills and the need to discover unity within the individual as well as in mankind in general.

The original work was carried out on split-brain patients, drawing the researcher to the conclusion that these people had two separate mental units, two separate spheres of consciousness. Now it has been shown that the two hemispheres in normal people also specialize and it is as if we had two brains, two spheres of consciousness with different modes and functions. The scientists who have studied these two spheres of consciousness in normal as well as split-brain patients describe very different functional capacities. The left hemisphere is verbal and descriptive; its function is predominantly logical, rational and comparative. Thought in this hemisphere is linear, sequential and relative; it appears to relate the superficial aspects of what is being perceived, and it would appear that this hemisphere has constant activity. The right hemisphere is almost non-verbal and non-descriptive. Its function is predominantly intuitive, creative and artistic. Whereas the left hemisphere operates on a relative and comparative mode, the right hemisphere gives a perception which is holistic, unifying, spacious, with depth and inner perception. Whereas the left hemisphere is in constant activity, this other sphere of consciousnss is still.

Everyone has within him or her these two spheres of consciousness, but their availability varies from person to person. In the busy scientific West, most people are dominated by the ever-moving verbal left hemisphere with its rational, comparative manner of thought. The Western educational system tends to be orientated to the left hemisphere and science, which plays such a major role in Western communities, is based on left hemisphere thinking, analysis, rationalization and comparison. Of course, there are many individuals in the West who are intuitive, creative and artistic but they operate in a

Western society which is basically scientific and materialistic, utilizing rational left hemisphere thinking for planning and sequential manipulation of Nature's resources. The scientifically orientated West has been suspicious of the East, which emphasizes the importance of the other mode of consciousness. The East has not followed the same scientific development, is relatively inefficient in the production of material things but has a depth and perception not seen in the West, and the last decade has seen many Eastern teachers arriving in Western communities to teach methods which give access to the still, inner-perceiving, unifying mode of consciousness latent in everyone. To have access to a sphere of consciousness which gives stillness, depth and inner perception is to transcend the ever-moving logical mind and discover a new dimension of mind and a new concept of reality, expressed so well by Aldous Huxley.

> Each of us is potentially Mind at Large. But insofar as we are animals our business is at all costs to survive. To make biological survival possible, Mind at Large has to be funnelled through the reducing valve of the nervous system.

But, Huxley says, it is possible to by-pass the reducing valve, giving

> something more than, and above all something different from, the carefully selected, utilitarian material which our narrow, individual minds regard as a complete, or at least sufficient, picture of reality.

It is possible to by-pass the reduction of consciousness by responding to the centre in each of us which is neither verbal nor rational but has to do with an inner perception of that which is whole, complete and one. Everyone utilizes the functions of the right hemisphere, but in Western society the tendency to over-utilize the verbal, comparative left hemisphere tends to lead to left hemisphere domination, with reduced use of the right hemisphere except for creative and artistic activities. Those who are ruled by the left hemisphere find themselves in the company of a verbal, restless, unceasing commentator whose domination renders everything flat, sequential, divided and separate, so there is no space and precious little time. Meditation is a simple technique of reducing the dominance of the left hemisphere and

45

allowing the silent, right hemisphere to come into being. Then there is greater peace, space, depth, unity and consciousness. Meditation is not the only technique for reducing the dominance of the left hemisphere; for example, the Zen masters force their students to use the right hemisphere by questions such as, "What is the sound of one hand clapping?" Such a question cannot be answered by the left hemisphere.

One advantage of meditation is that unlike some of the more difficult and perplexing disciplines, it is easy and simple to practise in everyday life. When one comes out from the practice of meditation there is a sense of greater ease, of calm, stillness, space and more time. This change in our sense of time now has a rational explanation, the scientists indicating that the two hemispheres have different time modes. It was the physicist Robert Oppenheimer who spoke of these different time concepts in thought.

> These two ways of thinking, the way of time and history and the way of eternity and timelessness, are both part of man's efforts to comprehend the world in which he lives. Neither is comprehended in the other nor reducible to it . . . each supplementing the other – neither telling the whole story.

We still need our functional, rational, comparative, verbal left hemisphere thinking but, to live in harmony and comprehend the whole, one needs to utilize the other dimension of consciousness. Over-use of the left hemisphere produces imbalance, agitation, stress, conflict, disease, no real understanding, and a superficial existence with neither point nor purpose. The technique of meditation allows one greater access to that part of the mind which does not deal in movement, words and images. Quietening the dominant left hemisphere and allowing access to the stillness of the right, not only gives greater peace, clarity, unity, depth and inner strength, but also slowly and gradually this restores balance and harmony. Through this process, latent facilities are released and inner perception developed. All this is naturally available, and this natural process puts one in touch with inner being beyond the movements of mind and allows the development of higher levels of consciousness. It shows that there is a level of mind which is still and reflective, allowing creativity and discrimination based on inner perception.

Our normal waking consciousness, rational consciousness as we call it, is but one special type of consciousness,
whilst all about it, parted from it by the filmiest of
screens, there lie potential forms of consciousness
entirely different.

These words of William James reflect the fact that the deeper modes
of consciousness are neither difficult to find nor far away, one simply
needs a practical method of access to them. He who discovers consciousness in depth is firm, sure as standing on a rock; there is no fear,
no doubt; such a man has knowledge in HimSelf and is free. He
comes into contact with that which is ever the same. He simply uses
the organs of conscious perception which are available to him as his
birthright, understanding the words of William Blake:

If the doors of perception were cleansed, man would see
everything as it is, infinite.

To utilize the still, inner perceiving, unifying part of mind not only
gives practical benefits in everyday life but also opens up the possibility of comprehending the underlying unity.

There is one mind common to all individual men. Every
man is an inlet to the same and to all of the same. He that
is once admitted to the right of reason is made a free man
of the whole estate. What Plato has thought, he may
think; what a saint has felt, he may feel; what at any time
has befallen any man, he can understand.

(Emerson: quoted in *Lamps of Fire*, Ed. J. Mascaró)

Only in stillness of mind can this reflection of unity be caught. The
ever-moving aspect of mind cannot but operate in a world of relativity, of passing time, of what was or may be. Stillness of mind brings
apprehension of that which is eternal, adding to the world of relativity
a new dimension.

The secret of good living is to live always both in the
moment and in eternity: or, for this is the truer way of
putting it, to live in the moment as eternity and eternity
as the moment: the two, for anyone who has mastered the
secret, being one.

(Quoted by Victor Gollancz in *From Darkness to Light*)

Chapter 8

The Way of the Householder

Meditation means to me a new way of life, It is as though I have had a glimpse of the great secret of life. This is so compelling that one must forever pursue it. There is more and more to discover. This gives hope and freshness to each day. I realize too the unity between all men and that love is everywhere.

The sadness, uncertainty, despair which beset me at times are seen more and more to be but passing clouds.

The memories of past mistakes and wrong actions no longer hang over me and spoil the present.

(Civil Servant)

Meditation has brought "point" into my life whereas, before meditating, life seemed to have no point. It is not something I can put into words or explain – what this "point" is; but I can now say that life is richer, more joyful, with greater communication with my fellow human beings, in fact with everything around me, even when working in an extremely busy and active city.

I seem to have come to rest within myself and, at times, when activity seems greatest, I find myself remembering stillness which before was hidden and now has been uncovered.

(Graphic Designer)

Before I meditated I thought I was happy. Now I know what being happy means, and this gives much deeper satisfaction. The practice of meditation has brought clarity and serenity to some of my actions. The beginning of an experience of oneness with other people is another exciting discovery through meditation, leading me to want to know more of this. In general, meditation has opened my eyes.

(Housewife)

There is a feeling that something is growing within me. It is becoming stronger day by day. It is love, it is happiness, it is understanding. It is greater than my mind can comprehend, yet it grows on.

(Accountant)

Meditation develops efficiency of action, clarity of mind and warmth of heart; it is a way of developing the whole man; it is a way of unity. (When the word "man" is used in this context, it is speaking of mankind; it includes male and female, man and woman. The pronoun "he" relates only to this use of the word "man".) Meditation does not require retirement or withdrawal from the world, and is therefore sometimes called the Way of the Householder. It may be followed while the man maintains an active part in life. In fact, for the householder on this way, realization and discovery come outside meditation and during activity. While maintaining his place and responsibility in the world, he discovers that meditation opens up a path to Self-Realization, which is a way of unity and truth, to be realized in himself and in the world.

Some people who discover the simplicity and depth of meditation discover the unity and truth in one step. These are they who have a natural love for meditation. Others come to the deeper discoveries step by step. These steps are well charted and have been described in many ways. The simplest formulation is shown in this diagram:

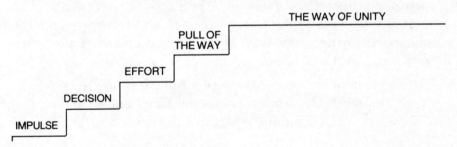

The first four steps are analogous to those which have to be taken towards any goal in life. For example, if a man wants to qualify as an accountant, and to work in the way that an accountant works, he must first have the *impulse* to take up accountancy. Then he must *decide* that this is the way he wants to go. Next, he must make *effort* towards achieving this aim. If he makes the right kind of effort, and finds that his chosen career is right for him, he then feels a *pull* towards working in that way. If he continues to work without losing direction, he qualifies as an accountant, and is set on his particular way.

On the path to Self Realization, the way is called the Way of Unity, for it leads to the discovery of the unity of the individual and the unity of all aspects of the universe.

On the way of unity, there are three more steps or stages. The first is called Self Consciousness, which is reached with the discovery of the unity in the man himself, and his ability to act in unity with all others.

The second step is marked by the widening of consciousness which brings knowledge of the same Self in everybody and everything.

The third step is described as full Self Realization. There are few fully realized people in existence at any given time, but this stage is a possibility for all human beings – it is, indeed, their goal.

This book, however, is principally for those who want to know how to take the very first step, or how to recognize what they may already be experiencing. So we turn back to the first four steps.

Impulse comes from within. It oftens manifests as a memory that there is more to life than meets the eye; an inner voice that may come in moments of quiet.

> Impulses of a deeper birth
> Have come to him in solitude.
> (A Poet's Epitaph)

So wrote Wordsworth of that which speaks to the poet in man. The impulse which leads to the search for truth and reality came to the contemporary writer Anne Gage at the age of twelve when she heard a voice say, "I AM".

> The experience never came again. But it is enough to stir me to action. I have discovered something I did not know existed. What is within? What am I? I will not rest until I know.

In her book *The One Work* she describes losing the direction of the impulse.

> I appeal to those who have gone before, who have shown the Way . . . But . . . there were two constant desires – the one for truth, the other for what I called life. Often I have mistaken one for the other and eagerly gulped up

experience, clenched in its fist, truth was forgotten and I
ran down avenues trying to remember and crying because
I had made the same mistake. Is there no other way?

Impulses can easily be covered by all the pulls we experience towards this and that, arising from the more superficial levels of the mind and senses, which keep a man from discovering anything new, so that he is constantly on the conveyor-belt of passing time. A whole life can thus pass by without inner significance.

> Tomorrow, and tomorrow, and tomorrow,
> Creeps in this petty pace from day to day
> To the last syllable of recorded time,
> And all our yesterdays have lighted fools
> The way to dusty death. Out, out, brief candle!
> Life's but a walking shadow, a poor player
> That struts and frets his hour upon the stage
> And then is heard no more: it is a tale
> Told by an idiot, full of sound and fury,
> Signifying nothing.

Shakespeare understood how the impulse could be buried or perhaps briefly acknowledged and then covered over. In his thirty-third sonnet, the masking of the inner light is likened to clouds obscuring the sun.

> Even so my sun one early morn did shine
> With all triumphant splendour on my brow;
> But, out alack! he was but one hour mine,
> The region cloud hath mask'd him from me now.

It is writings such as these, along with the great scriptures, which feed the buried memory and the impulse within. Reminders from a poet are particularly useful, for they emphasize the fact that this impulse arises from beyond the logical surfaces of the mind and is not something to think, argue or rationalize about.

Once the impulse arises, the individual must make a firm *decision* to act upon it, whether he can justify it logically or not. This may not be so easy, because of those mental habits which make most of us unwilling to commit ourselves to something unknown. At this point the experience of others who have trodden the path is helpful.

Dag Hammarskjöld, Secretary General of the United Nations, wrote in the diary found after his death:

> I don't know Who – or what – put the question, I don't know when it was put. I don't even remember answering. But at some moment I did answer *Yes* to Someone – or something – and from that hour I was certain that existence is meaningful and that, therefore, my life in self-surrender had a goal . . . From that moment I have known what it means "not to look back", and "to take no thought for the morrow".
>
> Led by the Ariadne's thread of my answer through the labyrinth of Life, I came to a time and place where I realized that the Way leads to a triumph which is a catastrophe, and to a catastrophe which is a triumph . . . As I continued along the Way, I learned, step by step, word by word, that behind every saying in the Gospels stands *one* man and *one* man's experience . . .

Some find the way themselves, but for most *decision* acts as a springboard to the initial effort of finding somebody, or some organization, to show the way. After that, the *effort* is the simple one of putting instructions into practice, regularly. In the case of meditation, once one has had the inner experience, it is not difficult to succumb to the *pull* of that way of working, for the experience is of something natural and known already. Now there is some inner light, but there are still outer pulls and inner clouds that mask the light. One has to wait until the next stage of inner unity for the way to be clear and the outer pulls to lose their distracting power. Once on the way, separateness and inner conflict disappear. Anne Gage after many outer pulls discovers the way, the way back.

> I have come from the Unity into the separateness of existence, yet there is a way back to Unity through discarding of self and finding of Self.

The inner meaning of the first four steps is found in individual practice. For example, decision, which we have described as the decision to embark on meditation, may return daily when one sits down to practise. Always, there has to be the decision to follow the simple instructions, to go that way, and to leave imaginings behind. Equally, right effort may need to be made at every session, which means consciously abandoning wrong effort – the temptation to make things more difficult for oneself. And at every practice the meditator can experience the pull of the way, which is the attractive power of the place of peace and unity which he will meet within himself. Provided only that he holds direction, the way to unity pulls of itself.

In the early stages, it is easy to lose the sense of unity and inner stability. It is as if one runs down the ladder again and has to await a fresh impulse. This works quickly and surely for the meditator who sits down to practise regularly. Thus, within the big external movement of impulse, decision, effort and pull, the pattern is repeated inwardly again and again, in the movement up the steps towards the platform which represents the way itself. This may become a way of life, for once established in unity a man stands on a platform of stability and inner being. He develops consciousness which transcends relative change. Techniques become secondary, and he is led and guided by the presence of that which is ever the same.

The Way of Unity – the way for the householder – develops *a whole man* while he remains in the world. Unity develops and embraces diversity and relativity. These are present together, like cells of the body, which are separate from each other but are yet contained in the total unity of the body, within which each plays its part for the good of the whole. Loss of this sense of wholeness gives rise to inner conflict, tension and a feeling of separation. Developing the whole being restores the sense of completeness, reducing inner conflict.

Many teachings refer to the three basic types of men: men of action, men of intellect, and men of devotion. These three aspects of being are in everyone, but one of them tends to predominate. There are ways of inner development which utilize and develop the predominant centre, often requiring hard discipline and retirement from worldly activities. The way of Self Realization opened up by meditation not only utilizes the predominant centre, but also gradually strengthens all three. This way of development is sometimes called the Fourth Way or the Way of the Householder, indicating that this way of inner development requires no withdrawal but is found through daily activities and life as it is lived in the world.

Chapter 9

Man's Constant Search

Meditation is union. To meditate is to be *one*. This *one* has been described in many ways. It is Our Father which art in heaven; it is the Self that lives in the hearts of all; it is Universal Truth; it is the Ultimate Reality; it is the Ātman; it is the Cosmic Intelligence; it is the *Nous*; it is *Brahman*; it is the Lord of All; it is the Omnipresent; it is *Jehovah*; it is *one*,

The experience of unity, of being *one*, is also variously described. It is *nirvana*, or *samadhi*, or dissolution, or full realization.

The message of this book, therefore, is not something new. It is as old as man himself. This *one* underlies all relative experience; and the constant search of man to discover and connect with that which lies beyond relative experience has been expressed throughout recorded history.

This chapter is devoted to some of the many expressions of this search, expressed variously according to time and place, culture and tradition. Some people are delighted by one idiom, some by another. Here is a simple anthology of expressions of the search for *one*.

o   o   o

Truth is within ourselves; it takes takes no rise
From outward things, whate'er you may believe.
There is an inmost centre in us all,
Where Truth abides in fullness, and around,
Wall upon wall, the gross flesh hems it in,
This perfect, clear perception, which is truth.
A baffling and perverting carnal mesh
Binds it, and makes all error; and to know

Rather consists in opening out a way
Whence the imprisoned splendour may escape
Than in effecting entry for a light
Supposed to be without.

(Robert Browning)

Once upon a time, or rather, at the birth of time, when the Gods were so new that they had no names, and Man was still damp from the clay of the pit whence he had been digged, Man claimed that he, too, was in some sort a God.

The Gods weighed his evidence, and decided that Man's claim was good.

Having conceded Man's claim, the legend goes that they came by stealth and stole away this Godhead, with intent to hide it where Man should never find it again. But this was not so easy. If they hid it anywhere on Earth the Gods foresaw that Man would leave no stone unturned till he had recovered it. If they concealed it among themselves they feared Man might batter his way up even to the skies.

And while they were all thus at a stand, the wisest of the Gods said: "I know. Give it to me". He closed his hand upon the tiny unstable light of Man's stolen Godhead, and when that great hand opened again, the light was gone.

"All is well. I have hidden it where Man will never dream of looking for it. I have hidden it inside Man himself."

(Rudyard Kipling (?): The Thing Hid Inside a Man)

Begin to search and dig in thine own field for this pearl of eternity that lies hidden in it; it cannot cost thee too much, nor canst thou buy it too dear, for it is *all*; and when thou hast found it thou wilt know that all which thou hast sold or given away for it is as mere a nothing as a bubble upon the water.

(William Law: The Eternal Pearl)

In this body, in this town of Spirit, there is a little house shaped like a lotus, and in that house there is a little space. One should know what is there.

What is there? Why is it so important?

There is as much in that little space within the heart, as there is in the whole world outside. Heaven, earth, fire, wind, sun, moon, lightning, stars; whatever is and whatever is not, everything is there.

If everything is in man's body, every being, every desire, what remains when old age comes, when decay begins, when the body falls?

What lies in that space does not decay when the body decays, nor does it fall when the body falls. That space is the home of Spirit. Every desire is there. Self is there, beyond decay and death; sin and sorrow; hunger and thirst; His aim truth, His will truth.

(Chhāndōgya-Upanishad)

Whither shall I go from thy spirit? or whither shall I flee from thy presence?

If I ascend up into heaven, thou are there: if I make my bed in hell, behold, thou art there.

If I take the wings of the morning, and dwell in the uttermost parts of the sea;

Even there shall thy hand lead me, and thy right hand shall hold me.

If I say, Surely the darkness shall cover me; even the night shall be light about me.

Yea, the darkness hideth not from thee; but the night shineth as the day: the darkness and the light are both alike to thee.

(Psalm 139:7–12)

I laugh when I hear that the fish in the water is thirsty.

Perceivest thou not how the god is in thine own house, that thou wanderest from forest to forest so listlessly?

In thy home is the Truth. Go where thou wilt, to Benares or to Mathura; if thy soul is a stranger to thee, the whole world is unhomely.

(Kabir)

Falsehood turns from the way; truth goes all the way; the end of the way is truth; the way is paved with truth. The sage travels there without desire.

Truth lies beyond imagination, beyond paradise; great, smaller than the smallest; near, further than the furthest; hiding from the traveller in the cavern.

Nor can penance discover Him, nor ritual reveal, nor eye see, nor tongue speak; only in meditation can mind, grown pure and still, discover formless truth.

(Mundaka-Upanishad)

56

But what if man had eyes to see the true beauty – the divine beauty, I mean, pure and clear and unalloyed, not clogged with the pollution of mortality and all the colours and vanities of human life – gazing on it, in communion with the true beauty simple and divine; remember how in that communion only, beholding beauty with the eye of the mind, he will be able to bring forth, not shadows of beauty, but its truth, because it is no shadow that he grasps, but the truth. And he will give birth to true virtue and nourish it and become the friend of God, and be immortal as far as mortal man may.

(Plato)

> There is a reality even prior to heaven and earth;
> Indeed, it has no form, much less a name;
> Eyes fail to see it;
> It has no voice for ears to detect . . .
> It is not mind, nor Buddha;
> Absolutely quiet, and yet illuminating in a mysterious way,
> It allows itself to be perceived only by the clear-eyed.
>
> (Dai-o Kokushi: *On Zen*)

Let the man return into his own self, and there in the centre of his soul, let him wait upon God, as one who listens to another speaking from a high tower, as though he had God in his heart, as though in the whole creation there was only God and his soul.

(St Peter of Alcantará)

> I learn hereby of a work that is invisible and seems like rest.
> How few know of a teaching that is silence; of a work that is
> not work, and is peace.
>
> (*Tao Te Ching*)

Peace I leave with you, my peace I give unto you: not as the world giveth, give I unto you. Let not your heart be troubled, neither let it be afraid.

(St John 14:27)

When forced, as it seems, by thine environment to be utterly disquieted, return with all speed into thy self, staying in discord no longer than thou must. By constant recurrence to the harmony, thou wilt gain more command over it.

(Marcus Aurelius)

For this commandment which I command thee this day, it is not hidden from thee, neither is it far off.

It is not in heaven, that thou shouldest say, Who shall go up for us eaven and bring it unto us, that we may hear it, and do it?

Neither is it beyond the sea, that thou shouldest say, Who shall go
ver the sea for us, and bring it unto us, that we may hear it, and do it?

But the word is very nigh unto thee, in thy mouth, and in thy heart,
that thou mayest do it.

(Deuteronomy 30:11–14)

Empty yourself of everything.
Let the mind rest in peace.
The ten thousand things rise and fall while the
Self watches their return.
They grow and flourish and then return to
the source.
Returning to the source is stillness, which is the
way of nature.
The way of nature is unchanging.
Knowing constancy is insight.
Not knowing constancy leads to disaster.
Knowing constancy, the mind is open.
With an open mind, you will be openhearted.
Being openhearted, you will act royally.
Being royal, you will attain the divine.
Being divine, you will be at one with the Tao.
Being at one with the Tao is eternal.
And though the body dies,
the Tao will never pass away.

(Lao Tzu: *Tao Te Ching*)

With the mind right the individual self comes into flower. With the
self in flower the family becomes an ordered harmony. With the
families ordered harmoniously the state is efficiently governed. With
states efficiently governed, the Great Society is at peace.

Thus from the Son of Heaven down to the common people there is
unity: in this; that for everybody the bringing of the individual self to
flower is to be taken as the root. Since that is so, for the root to be out
of order and the branches to be in order is an impossibility.

(Confucius: *The Great Learning*)

But when his work was finished, the Artisan longed for someone to
reflect on the plan of so great a creation, to love its beauty and to
adore its magnitude. When, therefore, everything was completed

. . . He began at last to consider the creation of man. But among his archetypes there was none from which He could form a new offspring, nor in His treasure houses was there any inheritance which He might bestow on this new son, nor in the tribunal seats of the whole world was there a place where this contemplator of the universe might sit. Finally the Great Artisan ordained that man, to whom He could give nothing belonging only to himself, should share in common whatever properties had been peculiar to each of the other creatures. He received man, therefore, as a creature of undetermined nature, and placing him in the middle of the universe, said this to him:

"Neither an established place, nor a form belonging to you alone, nor any special function have We given you, O Adam, and for this reason, that you may have and possess, according to your desires and judgment, whatever place, whatever form, and whatever functions you shall desire . . . I have set you at the centre of the world, so that from there you may more easily survey whatever is in the world. We have made you neither heavenly nor earthly, neither mortal nor immortal, so that, more freely and more honourably the moulder and maker of yourself, you may fashion yourself in whatever form you shall prefer . . . To you it is granted to have whatever you choose, to be whatever you will."

(Giovanni Pico della Mirandola: Oratory on the Dignity of Man)

. . . Listen, son. You were born into the human-animal life of sense and nerve and will. But it is necessary that each man sometime be born again: into the consciousness of an even greater life. You have learned what in your ordinary animal existence is necessary for your earthly body. Now you must have awakened in you the instinctive need for self-perfection in your inmost spiritual being. You must be taught the laws of world-creation and world-maintenance, the laws of all life whatever form it takes: the living stones, the breathing mountains, the tall walking rain, as well as those of bird and fish, beast and man.

You must learn that each man has the debt of his arising and individuality of existence to pay; that this debt must be discharged as early and quickly as possible so that you, as I, as all, may assist in turn the most rapid perfecting of those other beings – those like ourselves, and those units of life advanced to the degree of self-individuality.

59

For only in this way can life progress, can life exist.

(Pueblo Indian in Frank Walters' *The Greater Life*)

Let not him who seeks cease until he finds, and when he finds he shall be astonished. Astonished he shall reach the Kingdom, and having reached the Kingdom, he shall rest.

. . . And the Kingdom of heaven is within you and whosoever knoweth himself shall find it. And, having found it, ye shall know yourselves that ye are sons and heirs of the Father, the Almighty, and shall know yourselves that ye are in God and God in you. And ye are the City of God.

(*Oxyrhynchus Sayings of Jesus*)

Lord Shri Krishna said: Why grieve for those for whom no grief is due, and yet profess wisdom. The wise grieve neither for the dead nor for the living.

There was never a time when I was not, nor thou, nor these princes were not; there will never be a time when we shall cease to be.

As the soul experiences in this body, infancy, youth and old age, so finally it passes into another. The wise have no delusion about this.

Those external relations which bring cold and heat, pain and happiness, they come and go; they are not permanent. Endure them bravely, O Prince! . . .

That which is not, shall never be; that which is, shall never cease to be. To the wise, these truths are self-evident.

The Spirit, which pervades all that we see, is imperishable. Nothing can destroy the Spirit.
The material bodies which this Eternal, Indestructible, Immeasurable Spirit inhabits are all finite. Therefore fight, O Valiant Man!

He who thinks that the Spirit kills, and he who thinks of It as killed, are both ignorant. The Spirit kills not, nor is It killed.

It was not born; It will never die; nor once having been, can It ever cease to be: Unborn, Eternal, Ever-enduring, yet Most Ancient, the Spirit dies not when the body is dead . . .

As a man discards his threadbare robes and puts on new, so the Spirit throws off Its worn-out bodies and takes fresh ones.

Weapons cleave It not, fire burns It not, water drenches It not and wind dries It not.

It is impenetrable; It can neither be drowned nor scorched nor dried. It is Eternal, All-pervading, Unchanging, Immovable and Most Ancient.

It is named the Unmanifest, the Unthinkable, the Immutable. Wherefore, knowing the Spirit as such, thou hast no cause to grieve.

(*Bhagavad Geeta*, Chapter 2)

> And it is with this belief and this knowledge that I say,
> You are not enclosed within your bodies, nor confined
>   to houses or fields.
> That which is you dwells above the mountain and
>   roves with the wind.
> It is not a thing that crawls into the sun for warmth or
>   digs holes into darkness for safety,
> But a thing free, a spirit that envelops the earth and
>   moves in the ether . . .
> But you do not see, nor do you hear, and it is well.
> The veil that clouds your eyes shall be lifted by
>   the hands that wove it,
> And the clay that fills your ears shall be pierced by
>   those fingers that kneaded it.
> And you shall see
> And you shall hear.
> Yet you shall not deplore having known blindness,
>   nor regret having been deaf.
> For in that day you shall know the hidden purposes
>   in all things,
> And you shall bless darkness as you would bless light.

(Kahlil Gibran: *The Prophet*)

Chapter 10

The School of Meditation

The School of Meditation was formed in 1961, shortly after Maharishi Mahesh Yogi brought meditation to Britain. Maharishi was a pupil of Shri Brahmananda Saraswati of Jyotish Pitha, who before his death was Head of the Tradition from which the method of meditation comes. He was succeeded by Shri Shantananda Saraswati and, since 1963, when contact was made with him, the School has received his guidance.

The Head of Tradition is known as Shankarāchārya, which simply means "Shankara the teacher". The original Shankara, who lived over two thousand years ago, was one of the greatest teachers and leaders of India and is still revered throughout that country. Four centres or "seats" were established to continue the tradition of Advaita Vedanta. Advaita means "not two", one without a second, unity without any separation. Such a way of thinking supports meditation as a practical method of discovering inner unity and dissolving all feelings of separation. For those who are interested in the knowledge behind meditation, evening meetings are held. At these meetings one may hear of the deeper aspects of meditation and the non-dualistic vedantic teaching, together with all other teachings which help to lead individuals to the discovery of unity and truth in themselves and in others. It should be emphasized that while we may speak of teachings, the knowledge of unity and truth is inner knowledge. All teachings are to help in finding the inner knowledge whereby an individual may recognize the truth and unity in the words of all great teachers.

These meetings are in addition to the personal guidance which is always available on meditation.

The School of Meditation is an independent self-governing organization, but its members have grown to appreciate the value of the guidance received from Shankarāchārya. Here are some of his words:

The rigorous disciplines of the past, which people often expect, have been done away with. This meditation system has now been created to relieve people of hard labour. This is made simple because ordinary men, in this age, cannot undergo strict discipline, by their own nature. So this simple technique of meditation is created to suit the calibre of ordinary men of this age. Once one has got properly started one should find further progress easy. But as far as the simplicity of the method is concerned, it is the result of a conscious experiment which has come to this stage. For example, when someone invented the printing system, it was very cumbersome at the beginning, but now it has developed to such a state that we take it for granted; we just never question it. Perhaps this simple meditation system will be taken for granted at a later stage.

o   o   o

Our tradition was made to be a beacon light from which many other religions and philosophies and methods have branched off. These, whoever holds this office has to put right, when in any of them the balance is upset at any time. It is not either religion or philosophy or yoga. It is a beacon light to set right what is wrong for all aspirants to spirituality.

o   o   o

You mentioned that you came from the West and find things a lot different in this land. There are outward differences between the two which do prevail. Going deep one would find that the system of meditation finds unity between east and west. Beneath the outward and multifarious cultural differences, there is no difference. The processes of thought, action and feeling conducive to meditation apply exactly equally to western and eastern man. The inner unity of Self accounts for inner unity of meditation. Consciousness is one for all. Although the physical and cultural variations and difference in ways of life prevail, there is no difference within. There is inner unity. This system

63

of meditation is to give rise to the inner unity of east and west and all. This simple device for development can equally be used by eastern and western man.

o   o   o

The necessity of doing meditation arises for the following reason: people see the physical world and it attracts their attention. This seems important to their mind. They cherish the idea that accumulation of its wealth, material and resources would blot out all difficulties or discomfort in life. Stimulated as they are by this single idea, they keep running fast and using every bit of their physical and spiritual selves to achieve that end. They run after prosperity and comfort. But when one thinks of it, one finds all this temporary, very momentary. There is that inner world which is a million times more extensive and far more stable. The most miraculous state of all is the state when all wealth, all comfort and everything seems to belong to one's own self.

o   o   o

The quicker pace of life is quickening everything and in this process the natural balance is being lost. The men on the path of knowledge and meditation work for peace and happiness. In doing so they become natural and thus enjoy everything. The scientist runs after effects; we look for the cause.

The physical world with all its laws is there and the physical faculties are also there to appreciate the physical laws within each of us. This is a common factor and common knowledge for which there are schools and colleges to provide such knowledge. The difference between this type of knowledge and ours is this: that if you find yourself disturbed and miserable, then beyond this physical world there is another world with its laws, which are known to us, and we can comfort you with them and lead to peace and happiness. We will also initiate you to make you able to go to the source of knowledge and energy with which you still further your life with peace, happiness, efficiency and precision.

A man can manage to live with less food, no house and very little clothing, but he cannot live without rest and the rest must be full. Rest is to give up, so he must give up in full. His physical world will crumble if this law is not obeyed.

The same applies to the other world, the spiritual world. One can go on looking for things and ideas which you think are useful and you go on accumulating them, but by accumulation of all this, when you are by yourself, you don't find peace because of lack of rest. Unless one has rest in love and happiness, one cannot survive, just as one cannot survive without sleep. This system is to provide the rest. To take people to bliss is simply giving them rest, to rest with the Self so that they may have new and fresh mornings of life. Without this, life is not peaceful and it is no wonder there is so much chaos in the world.

o o o

All the creatures in the world are running after the bliss, happiness. This is the great eternal chase. We run with our mind and also with the body. The body gets recharged if it gets rest, and there are many levels of rest. A running man gets rest by standing, the standing man gets rest by sitting, the sitting man gets more rest by lying down on the bed, and one gets the complete rest by having a deep sleep. This is how one gets the used-up energies back. Similarly, meditation is to give rest to the mind. The mind is also running for happiness. Some run fast and others faster. With meditation some just stand to have a little rest, some sit or lie down, and some are fortunate enough to dive deep and have the complete rest. According to the level of meditation, they derive their benefits. As one goes deeper and deeper one adds to peace and happiness. The test of a good meditation is the abundance of happiness available then and there. The test of a good deep sleep is that one gets up fresh and energetic. The benefits of the meditation are not only happiness but also that the physical body responds to efficient, precise work.

o o o

On the path to realization, we are not required to do anything, we begin to be what we are. In order to be what we are, we have to come out of what we are not. Those thoughts you are not, that intellect you are not, those feelings, those sensations, you are not. You are not that restless separate ego. Through meditation we give up all these things,

65

and when we reach the transcendental state, we begin to find out wha
we are. So, to begin to be what we are, we have not to give up anything
real. All the unreal world is created by our thoughts and ideas; give up
those and come to the real. And we do not have to do anything to give
up, we simply come to meditation and the meditation gives everything up for us.

o   o   o

When we talk about the first Shankarāchārya and the tradition of
Shankarāchārya, we do not mean that this tradition was produced
and created by Shankarāchārya. It was only made available through
him at a certain point in our history. The knowledge [of truth] does
not come from men at all. Neither from this Shankarāchārya nor
from any other leader of religion. The knowledge belongs to the
Absolute. These leaders only catch and expound it according to the
need of the time, place and people. They clothe the knowledge in a
fashion which suits the people living at the time and place. This is why
religions differ. Fundamentals are always the same, but details are
always different. Some say it in crude form and others say it in subtle
language, whereas a third might give a synthesis of the two. Humanity
is one, so human beings can have only one system of true knowledge
which has found different manifestations in different religions. No
one has created the true knowledge. It simply happens to pass
through certain individuals. There will never be a difference on the
principles, but the mode of expression will be different according to
the teacher and the need of the time and place. The true search is to
find the unity in diversity.

o   o   o

When the Realized Man walks, he just walks; when he sits, he merely
sits – nothing more. Each movement or stillness is appropriate to the
situation, and nothing else is going on within him.

(Question: What is the secret of his behaviour? How does he contrive to behave
like that in all the different situations of his life?)

He is true to himself. He behaves like himself, like no other person in
the world, and everything he says and does comes from himself.

Nobody else in the world can change that, and he relies on nobody else. He speaks in his own way, moves in his own way, out of his own experience, and therefore he acts naturally. All artificiality is gone, and so all conflict has gone. He just does whatever he has to do in a natural way.

o   o   o

Questions and Answers

Since the School of Meditation was founded in 1961, over 1,000 public meetings have been held, and some of the questions most frequently asked at these meetings are given here, together with the answers which are meant as guidelines or indicators.

Only full experience of meditation itself can finally answer many questions. Most of those which follow are dealt with more completely, directly or indirectly, elsewhere in this book. The reader should not be tempted, therefore, to hope that this chapter gives exhaustive explanations.

Q. **Is meditation like self-hypnosis?**

A. No, it has nothing in common with self-hypnosis. One does not fall into a trance in meditation. On the contrary, one is more fully aware of where one is and who one is than in normal waking experience. To meditate, one has to stay awake. The technique provides a focus for the attention, other than the daydreams and random thoughts which otherwise claim us. Following the simple instructions allows all the other activity in the mind to die down and come to rest; but one does not go to sleep, or fall into a trance.

Q. **Is meditation better suited to some types of people than to others?**

A. Meditation is successfully practised by people in all walks of life, young and old. Since the method does not depend on "intellect", one does not need to be learned or clever to profit from it. Those who get most from meditation are those who are prepared to practice sincerely and innocently. These qualities are not exclusive to any type or class.

Q. **How demanding is it?**

A. Not at all, really. Since there is no "doing" involved, and since most people have greater energy after a period of meditation, there is no loss there. Of course, some time has to be given, but at most this is but one twenty-fourth of a day, and the increased energy and efficiency that meditation makes available effectively means that there is no net loss of time.

Q. **Do you have to give up anything?**

A. This is rather like the previous question. The real giving-up is in the practice of the technique itself, where one can be led out of all that one is not: the thoughts, the dreams, the imaginings and the fears, the feelings which normally rule us, often, seemingly, against our will. Again, there is no "doing" in this, for it is a process that occurs naturally in the pursuit of the practice. It is not that these things are destroyed or that they go away, for after all it is they, it is said, which "make the world go round". But in meditation, for the two daily periods, one comes out of them. One comes free of their demands and no energy need be consumed by them. This is most necessary for, in truth, a man is not these things and he knows it. By letting them go in meditation and moving towards what one really is, a certain refreshment and clarity is found which, during the rest of the day, means that the meditator is more able to use these functions as instruments or servants, rather than being ruled by them.

In summary then, there is no giving up of anything real. The effect of meditation can be likened to allowing a bucketful of muddy water to be still and settle, so that the densest particles fall to the bottom, leaving the less dense substances to settle on top of them , until finally the water above is left pure and clear. Man is really that water, containing everything else but needing the stillness to reveal his true nature.

Q. **Is much discipline required?**

A. The first aspect of practising meditation which could be called "discipline" is in doing it regularly twice a day. After a very little regular practice (and there is *no* need to adhere to particular times each day) this can become as natural as sitting down to meals or going to bed at night. Similarly, staying at the practice for the given period on each occasion soon becomes equally natural. Thirdly, it is essential that, when one finds the mind wandering on to thoughts (as it is bound to do from time to time), one brings it back to the simple technique quite gently and without attempting to fight the thoughts. Continuing the analogy of meals, this is rather like eating just what is in front of you, rather than eating from other plates on the table.

As can readily be seen, these "disciplines" are easy and can be followed spontaneously, especially as putting them into practice just a little leads to such enjoyment as meditation can give. There is positively no place in meditation for the rigorous disciplines which some other systems entail.

Q. **Are there any failures?**

A. Some of the people who take up meditation do not continue to practise, although quite a number of these subsequently return even after the space of several years. A common cause of people giving up the practice is some significant change in their personal circumstances occurring before the practice has become established and which tends to overshadow it. A man may move house, get married, take a more demanding job, all of which may so fascinate him that he puts regular practice to one side. Very often then, his personal experience (pressure, tension, strain, etc.) will revert back to the condition which prevailed before he began meditation; but the memory of meditation and its benefits will now be stronger. When the impulse to meditate arises again, he quickly goes back to it. The point about this question is that practice is always needed just as it is for the violinist or painter. And the practice must be true; a person may sit for the required period, dwelling in imaginings with no benefit. But this is not the failure of meditation; it is failure to meditate. When the practice is sincere and according to the instructions given, there should be no failure.

Q. **Isn't it selfish? Aren't there more important jobs to be done in the world?**

A. To answer the second part of the question first: there is no more important job that any individual can do in the world than to put his own house in order, to discover who he really is, and what is his purpose. Societies are made up of individuals and no society can change until the individuals in it change. If we are looking for important jobs to do, we must start work on ourselves. Meditation gives us this great opportunity. It is a practical method of setting to work on ourselves, by which we are freed from all the second-hand ideas which usually fill our heads and we are able to establish contact with what is real and permanent in us, unaltered by the ups and downs of day-to-day life. Beneath all the movement of thoughts and sensations, the mind is still. Little is known of this part of mind in ordinary life but, when it is found in meditation, it is known to be the source of all creativity. A man who could find how to work from this stillness and from his real, permanent and true self would be an enormous power for good in society.

As for it being selfish, it is found without exception by those who meditate that selfishness and the preservation of one's own separateness are merely the product of illusory thinking. Selfishness just melts away in the light of meditation and one finds in its place a spontaneous warm-heartedness towards others and a natural desire to work with and for them.

Q. **Can anything so simple do this?**
A. The simplicity of the method is due to the great skill and knowledge of those men who devised this method of meditation. They have made it possible to avoid the harsh disciplines of other ways and to go straight to the heart of the matter, so that ordinary people may have the opportunity of realizing themselves, while continuing to live a normal life in the world.

Many people have tried the method since it was first introduced into this country and have found it quickly assumes a place of central importance in their lives, as a source of comfort, strength and confidence.

Q. **My friends like me as I am; do I not risk alienating them if I seem to be trying to alter my personality?**
A. What we are really, deep down, is unalterable. Most people feel this instinctively. What we show to the world, however, on the surface, may vary from day to day, hour to hour, minute to minute. It is affected by our moods, the weather, the news, and a host of other daily circumstances. We may have noticed, too, that we have a different personality for different people: one for the boss, another for those who work for us, and yet another for our family.

What meditation does is to reach down to that essential part of ourselves which never changes, to bring this out into daily life; to clear away all the layers of artificiality, so that when we speak it is really us and not some idea of what we should be like. What could be more natural than to be oneself?

One thing you may be sure of: the man who works for this will never lack friends. The world is yearning for men who know themselves – they are welcome everywhere.

Q. **If you become more placid, doesn't life become boring? Do you lose your drive?**

A. The stillness one finds in meditation, and which one is then able to carry into daily activity, is not the same thing as inertia. Placid is hardly the right word to describe it. It is a stillness, full of potential, very much awake, but restful. With the mind in this still but alert condition, one is much better able to respond to the many and varied requirements made of us in daily life. One finds oneself more spontaneous, natural, restful, and actions themselves are cleaner, more purposeful, precise. With the mind still and alert, one sees much more of what goes on and one is less absorbed by daydreams and inner conversations. Far from becoming boring, life takes on a new freshness; greater depths and significance are revealed in a way one could not have imagined. Life becomes a great adventure.

Do you lose your drive? As the previous answer showed, all that one loses is what is artificial, what is untrue. What we really are is always the same, never changing; so one need not fear that one will lose something that is real or of value, and certainly not the drive or energy with which to engage in life's activities. In fact, the opposite would be more true – one knows increasingly what the best in life is and one stands out for that with more assurance and strength.

Q. **Doesn't it make you feel superior?**

A. Not at all. It makes you more yourself. In the process, ideas about being superior just fade away. People find that as they become more themselves, they discover a greater unity in all things. This leads to a natural sympathy with others, just the reverse of that separate, false feeling of superiority.

Q. **Is meditation fun?**

A. The practice of meditation is certainly enjoyable. It is a rest for the mind and afterwards one feels refreshed and alert. It should not be thought of as hard work, for the effort is very small, "the effort of no effort", as we mentioned before.

People who meditate find they get more enjoyment out of life. Usually the mind is clouded by thoughts and feelings, so that one does not appreciate to the full all the diversity of life as it unfolds before us. Meditation helps to dissolve this cloud and bring mental clarity, so that one begins to enjoy more and participate more fully in life.

Q. **Will it change my life?**

A. Meditation will not change the events that befall us in our lives; but it can change the way we react to these events. Ordinarily, habit plays a large part in our actions, so that similar situations produce the same reaction in us, with little chance of anything new. Thus our lives tend to run on lines dictated by the habits of thought and action built up over the years. Much of this habit is useful but if, as is often the case, it dominates, then things seem stale and we quickly become set in our ways and enter a premature old age. Meditation can dissolve these gross encrustations of habit and restore to us the ability to act spontaneously in whatever situation we find ourselves. Everything then seems fresh, and our actions are more appropriate since they spring from the needs of the situation, not from unconscious habit. Thus, the possibility of change may enter our lives and new horizons of fulfilment may open to us.

Q. **When can I expect to see results?**

A. It is difficult to be specific, because people benefit from meditation according to their particular needs and these are all different. In general, many people find within a few days that on the purely physical level they have more energy, feel more relaxed and are happier. In the longer term, most people find their general health improved and sleep better. Meditation works not only at the physical level, but at all levels of our being, although results at the deeper levels may take longer to emerge.

What is probable is that you will be unlikely to spot the more significant results of meditation within yourself until after some time, although they are obvious to others. Being quite natural, they develop or grow without our noticing, just as our fingernails and hair grow continually, without our being aware of it. Of course, we do have the benefit of these results whether we have noticed them or not.

Q. **Does it help to have a "religious" cast of mind? Does it help not to have a "religious" cast of mind?**

A. The most helpful attribute for meditation is an open mind, free from preconceived ideas, allied to a willingness to follow instructions simply and innocently. Meditation is not a religion and does not depend on belief for its effectiveness, so that the possession of a "religious cast of mind" is not of any significance. On the other hand, such people are not at a disadvantage, provided they are able to keep an open mind and follow the instructions given. Indeed, many people who have taken up meditation from a religious background and upbringing have found new and deeper significance in their faith.

To meditate effectively, all that is necessary is that one follows the simple technique and the instructions one has been given. If this is done sincerely, there is no room for thoughts, religious or not. The aim of meditation is to realize who one is. The man who knows this is beyond belief and unbelief.

Q. **Is prayer akin to meditation? If I find prayer helpful now, is it likely that I will find meditation more helpful?**

A. Meditation is not like ordinary petitionary prayer, although there is some similarity with the practices of some of the Christian mystics of the past. Contemplation in the religious sense is also often confused with this meditation, but the two are quite dissimilar.

Meditation asks for nothing. One just uses the method to turn the mind in the direction of stillness, losing interest in all else. One answers one's own prayers on this journey, for the stillness is full of strength and confidence. Once this source of strength within oneself was discovered, the need of petitionary prayer would probably decline.

Q. **How do I know that my real self is good? Might I not, through meditation, discover that I am basically a bad person?**

A. This cannot be so. The real self is like a sun within you. It is the source and sustainer of life, without which nothing could exist. Just as the light and nourishment of the sun can be masked, so can the self be masked by negative thoughts and ideas about ourselves; but they are no more than a mask or covering. The sun continues to shine beyond the darkest clouds and, similarly, the self cannot be extinguished, however negative our behaviour. Without the self, there would be no thoughts of any kind; so it is simply a matter of going further than thoughts and getting to the source beyond all the qualifications. The technique of meditation is designed to do this; to take one beyond the usual relative values to unity with the real self.

Individual Experience : some more examples

Chartered Accountant:

Meditation gives a clearer direction to my actions. Tasks such as washing up or adding up figures can now be done with purpose.

I find that meditation is progressive in its benefits although the practice remains simple. When taking it up two years ago, I thought I would gain a greater peace of mind and a clearer meaning to life. In some measure I now experience these.

Shorthand Typist:

Fatigue or absent-mindedness has less effect on me if I do the exercise regularly, and outside events and emotions do not so easily gain control over my thoughts. It tends to be fairly easy to repossess oneself without any strong effort. Because the mind is more still, I have a better perception, I think, of what goes on around me. I still feel there is a great deal of room for improvement.

Trainee Teacher:

Before I began the practice of meditation, I spent many years under psychiatrists talking about my thoughts, feelings and sensations. Now through meditation I have experienced the unreality of all this movement by reaching a point in the mind which is still, indifferent and limitless, so that the thoughts, feelings and sensations seem to be floating on a surface without any conflict and eventually just dissolve.

During the day when things can become hectic and difficult, I am more able to allow the movement to go on and not be involved in the same way as I used to be, and sometimes just to smile at it all.

Research Biologist:

I have come to see meditation as a psychological discipline of immense value in quietening the mind, enabling the really important things to come to the surface, and generating energy to concentrate on one thing at a time – of great value to a biologist who has to deal with so many variables. The inner calm and cheerfulness which it develops are of particular value when dealing with other people – especially with difficult ones!

Radio and Television Mechanic:

It is simple really. Since I have been meditating I seem to be more in touch with my senses, therefore getting a much clearer impression of the outside world. There seem to be less diversionary thoughts about and those that I am aware of do not have the grip they used to; even ideas that one was completely ruled by and caused a lot of pain, one can smile at and just turn out to the world. The world is a much nicer, saner place now. It is not that it has changed at all really. It is just that one sees it from a different point of view. I can understand so much more now; things that used to confuse me do not any more; one can see into things a bit more, even to the extent of seeing life as just a game. Seeing this brings a lot of freedom and rest; all the anxieties vanish. Even when I am caught up with thoughts and feelings, it does not usually last long because suddenly one remembers; it makes you smile.

Building Works Supervisor:

I have a different set of values, not subject to or influenced so much by the pressures of today, but influenced by an increasing "better or good" motivation from within myself.

When I started meditation I stopped drinking, not a hard-fought battle; but because the need to drown my problem was no longer there, the tension had gone out of my life; I still had my problems but I had put them in perspective.

Meditation touches all parts of me, everything I do, all is changing.

Housewife:

It is not easy to express profound joy and gladness towards all and how much more simple it is to enjoy life and its wonders through harmony and daily practice of meditation.

Violin Teacher:

Meditation has become part of my very existence. I wonder

now how I could have lived without it over all these years because it has brought me into a complete understanding of other people's motives for doing certain things which in the past seemed very offensive to me. In playing the violin I have gained greater precision and control, and a greater ability to remain unaffected by anxiety over difficult passages. And in teaching, I have found myself able to understand more easily the fundamental problems behind a pupil's difficulties. For example, I have one pupil whose rhythm is often unsteady because she is anxious and tense; when I can help her to relax, she is able to play perfectly in time.

Above all, there is the knowledge that I have an inner source of strength which will be sufficient to deal with any problems I may meet.

Housewife:

The most important thing about meditation is, however imperfectly practised, it works.

Management Consultant:

I think I can detect the beginning of certain effects which could be listed as follows:
1. A sense of repose and a quietening of the jangled nerveendings.
2. A physical relaxation of the muscles and an awareness of the constituents of one's own body.
3. A rather curiously heightened awareness of the external world, particularly sounds.
4. An improved sense of proportion as to the relative importance of many of the things encountered in daily life.

Sub-editor:

"You are fantastically tense", the doctor said, when I saw him about a persistent headache, and he prescribed a tranquillizer. That was during the years when, imprisoned in my self-absorption, I suffered mental agonies over things like whether I was wearing the right clothes or ought to have shaken hands . . . Eleven years of meditation have not abolished all the tensions, but the difference is immeasurable; and I have learned that in the midst of difficulties, there is strength, and at the heart of turmoil, there is rest.

Solicitor:

Meditation has no exact definition or form and it does not repeat itself at any time one meditates. It is a reflection of the inner depth, as a peaceful experience of the mind, related to the ever-changing level of consciousness. It is a stillness which intermingles with an effortless flow of movement like the stillness of the sunrise which is never static.

Housewife:

Sometimes, not invariably, there is a sense of joyful serenity with a heightened awareness, a kind of vigilant attention which returns at intervals during the day.

Secretary:

From the beginning, meditation connected with a memory deep inside; it felt a natural thing to do, as if I had been doing it all my life.

Civil Engineer:

Meditation puts you in touch with yourself. All the surface things, the changing moods, ideas and circumstances, all the trivialities of life tend to take you away from yourself. But in meditation you leave these things alone as best you can and come back to yourself. It is like a thread which is always constant although everything else changes.

In fact, of course, this thread has always been there and it is rather that through meditation one discovers it and keeps in touch with it. I think when you first start to meditate you tend to look for change, but the change you look for is really on the surface. Things do change, but for me the main thing is this discovery of what is constant, this daily coming back to yourself.

Apprentice Potter:

The simple act of coming to rest twice a day helps me do three things: to put the rest of the day's activities into clear perspective, to strengthen the ability to be at peace, and ultimately to act more as a "whole" man. The practice reminds me of the fact that there is within me, as in everyone, a centre which is the ultimate source of my wellbeing and to which I must constantly return in order to draw strength.

In sum, meditation means for me a daily acknowledgement that any true identity lies not in my ego and its tiny world, but in something far greater and deeper – the unity that embraces all and everything.

Greek Teacher:

It gives me peace and although I live alone I never feel loneliness.

Medical Book Editor:

"When man finds invisible, nameless, homeless, shapeless, invulnerable rock, he is no longer terrified". Living as though on brittle ice over unfathomed depths of fear, one dare not look down. Finding the rock, knowing its underlying presence, one need only trust that knowledge and let go.

How do we miss the rest
Which is everywhere?
It is as though we said,
"I will not breathe the air".

How do we lose the joy
As boundless as the light?
It is as though we said,
"Let there be night".

How do we doubt the grace
Which holds us in its care,
When rest and joy and peace
Are everywhere?

Musician:

The still but overflowing reservoir of creative energy continually informs one's work. The outside world would have me believe that this or that fruit of labour is mine. Thanks to meditation for the steady reminder of the true source of "my" talents.

79

Company Director:

I used to imagine what I would wish for if granted one wish. It was always "peace of mind".

Very struck by the calm and simple happiness of the one person I know who was not affected by the turmoil and strain of City life, I started to question her. She told me that meditation had freed her from the involvement of unnecessary worries and, during our talks, I became aware of a completely different kind of thinking, another set of values. I realized how little I had questioned the attitude and ideas with which I had grown up. She gave me a telephone number of the school to which she went, but it was some years before the muddle and stress of my unhappy condition made me reach for the telephone and dial the number.

I cannot say that the state of mind I was in has *completely* disappeared. But I have now been meditating for three years and have recognized the condition to be merely a false way of thinking, a bad habit. The quiet periods of meditation twice a day have brought me out of a vicious circle that an uncontrolled mind led me into and, as the restless thoughts have subsided, I have seen my errors. Now, when the old habit starts again, I recognize it for what it is, and am able to control it.

Today, after some operations from illnesses, including cancer, which I believe I brought on myself, I am essentially calm and happy. On the way to my office I look at the trees, listen to the birds sing, feel the strength and life in my body as I walk.

People come to me with their troubles, the causes of which I can see so much more clearly than I could. I long to be able to tell them of meditating, but know that I must wait for their interest. I am beginning to understand so many things, now that the thoughts which prison us in misery so much have dropped away from lack of nourishment.

What meditation means to me is: that the one wish I thought would never be asked me has been granted. I now have "peace of mind".

Aircraft Radio Engineer:

Man enters this world into this or that society, possibly into

80

one of the 20 or more countries on this planet each claiming the right to wage war one on another. He find stockpiles of hydrogen bombs, poisons, "advanced" technologies, pollution, propaganda, lies, chaos, starvation, drought, disease, indignities, suffering. These countries, or powerful minority groups in these countries, are ready to use any means whatever to crush opposition and gain power. In these circumstances, it may be very difficult for man to avoid contributing to his own downfall.

He finds hundreds of religions or philosophies, often claiming that only theirs is the way. Also confronted by his disturbing desires, fears and ignorance, and by the very temporary nature of his body, a man may feel he could benefit from suitable guidance in order to remain of happy countenance and good cheer, or to discover his deeper nature and purpose and to live a useful life, evolving to a higher level of being.

A man is fortunate to find a teaching able to give proper direction and guidance. For this man, meditation seems to be a suitable Way.